THE WRITER'S GUIDE TO DEEP POV

THE WRITER'S GUIDE TO DEEP POV

CREATE REALISTIC CHARACTERS, SETTINGS, AND DESCRIPTIONS

S. A. SOULE

FWT

Published by FWT

The Writer's Guide to Deep Point-of-View (Book 2)
ISBN: 978-1530515448

Cover art by SwoonWorthy Book Covers

FWT appreciates its readers, and every effort has been made to properly edit this guidebook. However, typos do get overlooked. If you find an error in the text, please send us an email so the issue can be corrected. Thank you!

Typesetting services by BOOKOW.COM

For fiction writers who never give up on their dreams and always strive to improve their storytelling abilities...

Contents

Contents

INTRODUCTION

Dear Writer,

I've been writing most of my life, and even though I've studied the craft for years, I still love developing my skills as a writer, and I'm assuming since you purchased this book that you do too.

First I thought I'd share a little about myself…I have over fifteen years of experience on all sides of the publishing business. I was a Creative Writing major, and I owned an eBook publishing company where I edited over a hundred manuscripts. Then I worked as a developmental editor for another publisher, and in the last five years, I've even had the honor of editing books for a number of successful authors.

In the past, I've been traditionally published, and through a small indie publisher, and I've even self-published my work. Currently, I've written eleven fiction novels and eight nonfiction titles, but it wasn't until 2015 that I became a bestselling author, but the road to success has been a long journey. Many of my books have spent time on the 100 Kindle bestseller lists and some of my fiction has been chosen as top picks in the "Best Paranormal Romance" categories at several prominent review sites.

As requested from so many writers, I have written this companion book to my bestselling "*The Writer's Guide to Character Emotion*." This manual covers a whole new set of topics and provides step-by-step methods to deep editing techniques that will create gripping page-turners. Writers will learn how to create realistic dialogue, vivid settings and character descriptions, along with a strong, unique voice. Additionally, this handbook expands on how to master describing emotions, body language, and strengthen characterization with simple ways that writers can easily and quickly apply to their own writing.

In this guide, I also share some of the wisdom that I've gleamed from various workshops and online courses, along with the savvy advice from bestselling novelists and professional editors with whom I've had the pleasure to work with in the publishing industry. Plus, I've included insightful and inspiring quotes as encouragement.

This manual is not a "grammar do or don't" because mine is not the best, so please don't contact the literary police. Writers should use these tips as an arsenal of creative knowledge to include in their writer's toolbox. My goal is always for writers to come away with stronger writing and editing abilities that they can utilize in their own stories and give their audience a more personal reading experience.

Happy revising!

~S. A. Soule

DEEPER POV

Quote: "The difference between showing and telling can be set out in four words. Showing reveals. Telling explains." —*author, James Thayer*

In the early drafts of a manuscript, *telling* is expected. It is more important to get the story finished and the plot holes filled in, then to worry about if a writer is *showing* enough. It is during the revision stage of later drafts (more like draft five or six) when it's time to polish the storyline and start checking for red flags of *telling* and begin enhancing the characterization, along with the setting and dialogue.

Just stating that you need to "*dig deeper*" or having someone say, "don't show" can become confusing for a lot of writers. I think that's one reason that I wanted to share my knowledge and understanding of the Deep POV technique.

When writers are told to *show, don't tell*, they're frequently left without any step-by-step instructions on how to fix those problem areas in a story, and even when *not* to use Deep POV, so this guide should help shed some light on those issues.

The Deep POV method can be used in a lot of different ways besides the obvious ones, like *show emotions* or just *getting inside a character's head.* It can also create engaging dialogue, aid in describing characters and vivid settings through sensory details, and even strengthen characterization. We just need to understand *how* and *when* to apply it.

Showing merely means allowing the reader to deeply experience things for themselves, through the viewpoint and perception of a character. Deep POV is just describing everything that your character is feeling, observing, and identifying, along with whatever they're seeing, hearing, touching, and smelling, etc.

Throughout this guide, I have included examples to demonstrate how writers can avoid narrative distance in easy to grasp methods that can instantly improve anyone's writing.

*Please note that while all of the examples in my guidebooks have already been used (mostly in my own novels published under Sherry Soule), writers can turn almost any of these Deep POV examples into new, unique phrases that fit your own stories. The purpose of the examples that I provide are to get your own creativity flowing enough to come up with innovative ways to describe your characters and settings in your own distinctive style.

Let's check one example below...

SHALLOW: Sara realized that she had forgotten the baby at home.

DEEP POV: The thought struck her like a punch to the gut. She'd forgotten the baby at home!

Now ask yourself: which example caused more impact?

If Deep POV (showing) demonstrates detailed proof to the reader and permits them to obtain their own conclusions, than *telling* (stating the emotion or details) states a fact to the reader, telling them what to accept as true.

For instance, stating (telling the reader) that a character "realized" something, like she was late for work, is fine, but it is also somewhat shallow. Instead, a writer can *show* that the character is late by her rushed actions.

Please carefully compare these examples…

SHALLOW: I woke up and looked at the clock. I realized that I was late for work. I quickly showered and got dressed. Then I ran out the door.

DEEP POV: The morning light seeping through the window burns my eyes. Rolling over, I check the alarm clock. It's after eight.

Groaning, I throw back the blankets and rush into the bathroom. I hurry through a shower without washing my hair, and then brush my teeth. Back in the bedroom, I go to the closet and dig through the trendy garments, ripping clothes from the hangers. I glance at the clock again.

Ten minutes left before I miss my bus.

Needing a jolt of espresso, I yank on a dress and slip on my shoes. On my way out the door, I grab my purse and dash outside into the bright morning sunshine.

Could you perceive the difference? One is telling the facts in a bland way and the other is showing in a visual way.

Please study this example, where each sentence is *telling*…

SHALLOW: Kate <u>noticed</u> that it was getting late and it <u>looked very dark</u>. She <u>felt</u> cold. When she <u>saw</u> the shadows moving and <u>heard</u> a strange howling, she <u>felt scared</u>. She <u>saw</u> the house and she <u>started to run very fast</u> on the path.

Although, the first scene states the facts, it's inert and sluggish.

Here is a revision, where the same information is *shown*...

DEEP POV: The sky darkened and the wind wailed through the stiff branches on the pines. Kate shivered and hugged herself. The shadows shifted and the eerie howl of a wolf cut through the air. Her pulsed jumped. Kate spotted the porch lights glowing on the house and she sprinted along the path.

The second scene is much more vivid and visual, right?

In the second version the reader has all the same information–dark sky, the feeling of coldness, the fear, seeing shadows, hearing the howls, introspection, and started running—but the revised example is vividly alive because the reader has been given something to clearly visualize rather than reading a bland report.

Showing is more effort than just *telling*, but that is part of a writer's job during revisions.

Please compare these examples...

SHALLOW: He looked depressed.

DEEP POV: Tears slid down his pale face.

SHALLOW: He felt angry.

DEEP POV: He clenched his fist and his mouth formed a thin, flat line.

SHALLOW: She looked happy.

DEEP POV: She jumped in the air, clapping her hands.

SHALLOW: She felt envious.

DEEP POV: Her gaze narrowed and one side of her lip curled upward.

SHALLOW: He looked nervous.

DEEP POV: He chewed his bottom lip and fidgeted with his keys.

Most of the time, using Deep POV to *show* is much better than *telling* because of the experience it provides for our readers.

Now just to be clear, *telling* isn't always the wrong way to describe an emotion or reaction. It doesn't always indicate flat, shallower writing. Please take into consideration that "show, don't tell" is *not* a strict writing rule. As a matter of fact, none of the self-editing tips in this Deep POV book should be deemed as actual rules. There are going to be times in a writer's story when *telling* will be needed, because sometimes *telling* can be much more effective if done correctly. However, whenever a writer can use Deeper POV in their stories, they should treat their readers with respect by *showing*.

So just keep in mind that showing vs. telling is all about balancing the two concepts.

SHOW DON'T TELL

Quote: "Every creative writing student has heard the rule that you should *show*, not *tell*, but this principle seems to be among the hardest for beginners to master." —*author, Robert Sawyer*

First let me say this...I get it. I *really* do. Your book is like your baby, and you love it and you've poured your sweat and blood and tears into it. But sometimes writers need a take a step back and look at the writing from a reader's perspective...

I've found that a lot of novice writers that I've worked with get confused by the whole "show vs. tell" concept, and I admit that it used to confuse me, too.

A few months ago, one of my critique partners said that she thought writers could only use the Deep POV technique about 50% of the time. I disagree. I think it can be used anytime a writer wants to avoid *naming the emotion* or they use sensory details to describe a scene. And describing a character's body language, facial expression, actions, gestures, or tones of voice are just some of the many ways that writers can *show*.

Most of the time when writers do not apply Deeper POV, it creates narrative distance. This means that the reader has been distanced, or in some cases, jolted out of the story by author intrusion. The more *telling* a writer does, the more distance they put between the reader and the story, and the less involved the reader will feel to what's happening or a real connection to the characters.

And if readers aren't connecting to your characters, then you've got a major problem.

The number one reason that *showing* is more visual and appealing for the reader is that fiction is image focused, and *showing* usually generates a much more vivid image for the reader, rather than stating facts. Generally, *telling* doesn't produce a strong enough picture in the reader's mind, and it often causes author intrusion, which reminds readers that they are reading a story—and that's not something a writer ever wants.

Please study this example, where the sentence is *telling*...

SHALLOW: Caleb felt hot in his wool coat.

That sentence isn't an image the reader can effortlessly imagine. It's an ambiguous fact.

DEEP POV: Caleb swiped a bead of sweat from his forehead and shrugged off his heavy winter coat.

The revised sentence puts a very powerful illustration in the reader's mind.

If you read a ton of fiction like me, you'll notice *telling* in almost every published novel, some more than others, but that doesn't mean you should "tell" if you can *show*. I realize that some telling is mandatory in narrative, but not when you are describing the character's emotions or internal-thoughts. Those should always be shown by using the Deep POV technique.

Fiction is a creative art, and writers need to use descriptions and senses, and not simply state emotions or continuously give direct facts.

Please look at one example below...

SHALLOW: Jane was a beautiful young girl.

That sentence is a form of *telling*, and although the sentence states a fact, it gives a rather weak visual.

DEEP POV: Jane swept into the room and her delicate lilac perfume wafted in the air, tickling my nose. When she spotted me sitting alone, her pouty, pink lips lifted into an amazing smile that lit up her azure eyes. A thick mane of ebony waves fell over one shoulder, and to me she resembled a painting of a Greek goddess brought to life. For a moment, it felt like my heart stopped beating in my chest.

Now ask yourself: which description was more powerful and visual?

Now, I'm not suggesting that a writer show or describe *everything* in great detail because that would be overwriting and create pacing issues. The key is to understand the difference so writers can intelligently decide when to use Deep POV and when to just tell. Finding a balance is necessary.

Here are four easy to master tips on writing in Deep POV and red flags:

1) Writers should try to reduce as many filtering references as they can from their writing. Words such as *felt, saw, heard, smelled,* and *noticed*, etc. that tell the reader what the narrator felt or saw or heard or noticed instead of just stating it.

Always strive to find new and active ways to describe a character's emotional state, or allow your characters to convey their emotions through action, facial expressions, internal-dialogue, and body language.

2) Naming the emotion can become a bad habit that writers easily fall into. Writers create narrative distance and author intrusion when they deliberately or unintentionally insert shallower POV and telling sentences into their scenes.

Anything that directly states the narrator's thought, emotion, or mode of perception is considered *telling* the reader about whatever the character is experiencing.

Writers should have more respect for their readers by *showing* instead.

3) Be more specific when describing places, settings, people, clothing, objects, cars, etc. so you don't create a weak visual. The easiest way to stay in Deeper POV is to try to be much more specific whenever possible by including sensory details.

By writing with precise and detailed words, and avoiding vagueness, writers will remove most of the "tells" from a story and breathe new life into any scene.

4) One way to rid your fiction of shallow writing is to use the "look through the camera lens" method, which is an excellent tool for helping writers begin to notice any *telling* within a manuscript.

Imagine this: the character is standing behind the camera, and everything in the scene, is perceived through that POV character's eyes and then reported through their perspective.

But the camera can't view any of the five senses, like sounds, touch (the way something feels), smells, temperatures, or tastes. In addition, interior-dialogue—the character's internal thoughts and emotions—cannot be viewed by a camera, and so it is not (usually) considered telling.

***

There are times when *telling* will add to the rhythm of your sentence and it is simply necessary. Telling shouldn't be completely removed from your manuscript because that would be impossible and some of your prose could become particularly awkward.

Do I use filtering word/references on occasion?

Yes, because I mostly write in first-person POV and sometimes they are hard to avoid without creating awkward sentences. However, my advice is this: if you can rewrite the sentence without it and stay in Deeper POV, then do it. If some of the time you cannot, then go ahead and leave the shallow word in the sentence.

SENSORY DETAILS

Quote: "Place matters to me. Invented places matter more." — *bestselling author, Alice Hoffman*

Deeper POV removes bland storytelling by including sensory details and cranks it up a notch. It pulls readers deeply into the heads and hearts of our characters by allowing the story to be seen, experienced, and felt through the close-and-personal POV of the character.

If done correctly, Deep POV rids a story of unneeded phrases like *he thought, he knew, he heard, he smelled, he felt* (when it applies to emotions), *he wondered, he saw* that cause author intrusion. (Reminder: it is always okay to use shallow "telling" words in dialogue.)

Another huge advantage of applying the Deep POV method to your writing is offering the reader direct access to the character's moods, emotions, and perceptions. A character needs the ability to describe what she/he experiences as it occurs.

The most obvious way of *telling* and the number one red flag is to state the emotion or reaction. A better way is to show them through facial expressions, internal-monologues, and body language.

Please carefully compare these examples…

SHALLOW: The <u>smell</u> was awful and made me <u>feel sick</u>.

DEEP POV: I covered my nose and tried not to gag at the offensive stench.

Remember that "stating the emotion or reaction" for a reader is *telling*. The correct way is to *show* by describing what is unfolding in every scene by the use of action, "voice," dialogue, facial expressions, and the five senses, etc.

Writers can *tell* a reader that when Harry steps into the kitchen, he notices a stinky smell, but it is much more creative to *show*. Sometimes showing is more descriptive and wordy than just stating the facts, but where's the fun in that, right?

Please examine these examples…

SHALLOW:

When Harry went into the kitchen, he <u>noticed</u> there was a stinky <u>smell</u> coming from the sink. He <u>realized</u> that it <u>was apparent</u> that no one had washed the dishes in a very long time.

Sure, the shallow example gets to the point and states the facts, but let's be honest, it's bland and flat. Now compare this one written in Deeper POV.

DEEP POV:

The second Harry stepped through the kitchen doorway, a raucous odor wafted from the sink and made his nose wrinkle. *"Gross! When was the last time anyone cleaned the dishes?"*

The second example was more impactful, right?

Please examine these next examples…

SHALLOW:

While I changed into my gym clothes, I <u>watched</u> my best friend Dana carefully. I <u>noticed</u> that she <u>looked overly excited</u> to go work-out with weights and gym equipment. I <u>knew</u> something was going on with her, and I <u>decided</u> to find out.

That example was too bland and gives the reader a weak visual.

DEEP POV:

Grunting, I yanked on my tight gym clothes, while my best friend Dana was humming to herself and prancing around the stuffy locker room.

Once she'd finished dressing in a brand-new workout outfit, she turned to me all smiles. "Ready to get sweaty?"

"Since when do you like cardio?" I propped a hand on my love handle, protruding over the waistband of my sweats. "Are you crushing on that new trainer, Sergio?"

Dana twirled around like a ballerina in her glaring white tennis shoes. "Oh, yeah…"

***

Showing (Deep POV) makes your readers become even more emotionally invested in your wonderful story. One way to do that is for writers to use specific words to describe how things smell, how certain foods taste, how objects feel, how the setting sounds, and looks through your character's eyes.

Why keep your readers at arm's length, when you can pull them in close-and-personal?

Recognizing the difference between *showing* and *telling* is the most crucial skill a writer needs for stronger storytelling.

INTERNAL EXPOSITION

Quote: "Dialogue is a key part of any story and it's usually what readers find most engrossing. They might skim long descriptions, but when they get to someone speaking, that's where they'll get pulled back into the narrative."—*Moody Writing blog, mooderino*

Internal exposition is when a character is busy having a discussion inside their own head. It can provide vital information on how a character is reacting or feeling in regards to what's happening within the story, but it's a skill that if done incorrectly, often causes shallower writing.

Dialogue illustrates characterization quicker than any amount of exposition. If you disrupt the action and dialogue to include colossal chunks of detailed description or introspection, it will remove the reader from the story.

Yet, if I'm being honest, I have to admit that I've written a couple of bad novels, and had them published under a pen name many years ago. But that was long before I sharpened my writing skills and studied the art of fiction writing with a crazed intensity. I read articles on editing and revision, books on the craft, and studied style guides. I love learning new ways to improve my writing, so hopefully you gleam some insight from this chapter.

Long blocks of introspection can be dreary and slow down the pacing of a novel because it is passive, and often robs the reader of getting to know a character's personality and/or personal struggles by *showing* them.

While dialogue usually quickens the pace of the story, internal exposition slows it down.

So anytime a writer can revise introspection into dialogue, they should. Especially, when there are two or more characters in a scene.

Why have the character say it in his/her head, when it would be much more impactful to be shown in conversation?

Please carefully study this example...

SHALLOW: Henry said that he wanted to quit school. I wondered what Henry meant by that remark. Was he serious about dropping out of college?

DEEP POV: "I'm thinking about quitting school next semester," Henry said, shuffling his feet.

"Why would you do that?" I leaned back to stare into his face. "Are you serious about dropping out of college?"

Henry stared out the window and didn't answer.

***

The Deep POV example reveals more insight into the characters, rather than having the main character just thinking about it in his/her head.

Inner-monologue is one of the essential ingredients used to create a comprehensive story. Unfortunately, it's all too often one of the most misused elements in storytelling. Since internal-monologue is slower and can be boring for the reader, find ways to bring it to life through Deep POV, action, and dialogue. Don't let your character's mental babble (long blocks of introspection) go on for pages at a time without a break by either dialogue or action.

Whenever possible, I encourage writers to revise introspection (also known as internal exposition, interior monologue, inner-thoughts, or inner dialogue, etc.) into dialogue when there are more than two characters in a scene. I feel that dialogue is naturally faster paced and much more interesting to readers than long blocks of narrative.

I have included some examples on how to stay in Deep POV by turning boring exposition into attention-grabbing dialogue between two characters. (In the shallow example, I did not underline the obvious areas of shallower writing, but see if you can easily spot it.)

Please carefully compare these examples…

SHALLOW: I saw the pirate give me a mean look as he asked about his gold.

DEEP POV: The pirate's bushy brows furrowed. "Where be my gold, wench?"

SHALLOW: Martha McCray was angry and glared at me. I told her that I wasn't scared of her, but that was a lie.

DEEP POV: Martha McCray gave me the evil eye and I gave it right back to her. "You don't scare me," I lied.

SHALLOW: Damon wore a furious expression, and then he told Tyler that he was going to beat him up.

DEEP POV: Damon's eyes darkened and he rolled up his sleeves. "I hope you realize, I'm about to kick your ass, Tyler."

SHALLOW: Klaus stared at Stefan and he looked upset when he called him a liar and accused him of dating Caroline.

DEEP POV: Klaus gave him a hard, unblinking stare. "You lied! You *are* dating, Caroline."

SHALLOW: Emily felt angry. Why did he have to be such a jerk?

DEEP POV: Emily's lips flatten and she gets right in his face. "Why do you have to be such a jerk?"

SHALLOW: He seemed unsympathetic when he said that he would not help me with the corpse.

DEEP POV: His expression turned stony. "I'm *not* helping you bury the body. You're on your own this time."

SHALLOW: He was exasperated with the cops and demanded that they locate his daughter.

DEEP POV: He ground his teeth. "Find my daughter—*now!*"

SHALLOW: Amber looked indifferent when she complained that I always got my way.

DEEP POV: "Fine. Have it *your* way. You always do," she said, her tone laced with bitterness.

SHALLOW: Dorian was mad at her for asking if they could eat pasta again this evening.

DEEP POV: Dorian clenched his mouth tighter. "I do *not* want to eat pasta again tonight."

***

Writers never want the reader to feel removed from their story by too much introspection, instead of being deeply emerged within the fictional world that the author has worked so hard to create. Now I realize that writers can't turn all introspection into dialogue, but I encourage you to find clever ways to change the ones you can.

REALISTIC SETTINGS

Quote: "Don't tell me the moon is shining; show me the glint of light on the broken glass." —*playwright and short story writer, Anton Chekhov*

This chapter explains why Deep Point-of-View is one of the best editing techniques that you can use to create a realistic setting through sensory details without giving readers a weak or bland visual. The tools and tips in this section will demonstrate how writers can revise filter words used in shallower descriptions by transforming the setting into a much stronger visual.

By incorporating sensory details into a setting, along with vivid descriptions, writers can easily stay in Deeper POV. So, don't tell me that the house was on fire, instead *show* me the blaze and let me feel the heat on my skin.

Here are four simple techniques to make a setting more visual:

1) Make the landscape active by having characters interact within it.

2) Use color to add an extra depth to the scenery.

3) Make the setting a vital part of the scene.

4) Use the five senses to make the backdrop more realistic.

Sometimes writers need to simply and quickly convey details or information to the reader and move on, but if a writer applies Deeper POV on occasion, then they can bring the reader into the scene as intimately as possible.

For instance, when depicting a location/setting, describe things the way only your unique character sees them through their unique "voice" and include a few significant sensory details.

But when writers use "There was" or "There are" at the beginning of a sentence to describe an object or a setting, it creates a weak visual. These words add nothing to the scene, and sentences with these phrases can become wordy and flavorless.

Look at some examples…

WEAK: There are many witches living in the woods.

GOOD: Many witches live in the woods.

WEAK: There was a desk and a bed and lamp in the bedroom.

GOOD: The room contained an unmade bed, a dusty desk, and a tall brass lamp.

***

What usually draws a reader deeply into a story is the use of language and the way a writer describes a setting through the head and heart of their characters. One way to do that is to include a few of the five senses in every scene by describing them for the reader.

Please compare these next two examples...

SHALLOW:

There was a big table in the dining room and it looked like the wood was rotting. When I touched the surface it felt rough and dusty.

Now, the next example states the facts while giving readers enough of a visual to "see" the table in their mind's eye and experience the "touch" through sensory details without describing it in a boring way.

DEEPER POV:

A wooden table, its surface peeling away like brown bark, sat in the unused dining room. As my fingers trailed along its uneven surface, specks of dust coated my fingertips.

***

Quote: "...[if the writer] gives us such details about the streets, stores, weather, politics, and details about the looks, gestures, and experiences of his characters, we cannot help believing that the story is true." —author "The Art of Fiction" John Gardner

***

Showing is always much more powerful and explicit than just *telling* the reader, but it can often be more wordy. Yet I wouldn't let that hinder your use of this amazing tool. Sure, simply *telling* the reader can be a faster way to convey a lot of details about the setting, or things like a character's backstory and events; however, it is usually written in a way that is nondescript and slow and inelegant. It often creates long blocks of text without much "white space," or even "voice" within the narrative.

When readers see more than a page of thick text, they know it is straight exposition. That means no action or dialogue, which equals no forward movement of the plot. Which usually means: *boring*.

Have I made this offense? I'm sure I have, but I try very hard to avoid it.

My advice is to never push "pause" on your story to dump out long rambles of introspection or tedious facts about the setting. Although, I realize with some genres like high-fantasy or science fiction lots of world-building is needed, the descriptions can still be cleverly woven within the narrative.

Let's start with the description-dump. (In my guidebook, *The Writer's Guide to Vivid Scenes and Characters*, I provide even more examples on how to avoid doing an info-dump of description.)

When describing a room don't just catalog items or furniture like a monotonous list of inventory. To successfully create a visual scene, you need to balance the action of your characters with the description of the scene, along with the sensory details. Do not give your readers a weak visual through shallower writing.

(In the shallow example, I did not underline the obvious areas of shallower writing, but see if you can easily spot it.)

Please carefully compare these examples…

SHALLOW:

Sarah entered the room. There was a lamp, a couch, a tall grandfather clock and some letters on the table in the living room. Sarah saw some blood on the floor. She also observed a really bad smell. When she noticed the lifeless corpse, she got scared. When she heard the clock rang out the hour, she loudly screamed.

DEEP POV (sensory details):

Cautiously, Sarah tiptoed toward the dusty antique lamp and switched it on. Muted light illuminated the space. The stench of decay assaulted her senses as she weaved around the velvet sofa and past an oak table, which held a stack of unopened mail.

On the Oriental rug lay a bloody butcher's knife. Her eyes widened and her pulse thumped. Sarah backed up slowly into a towering grandfather clock. Her gaze followed the trail of blood over to a body, still and pale.

When the clock bonged midnight, she screamed.

***

Explanations of events are much more dramatic if your readers are directly involved and experiencing them along with the character. Readers may skim long pages of unbroken description; however, if it is slipped in as part of the action, then it is absorbed by the reader almost without being noticed, and enhances the scene. Always try to mix description with dialogue, actions, and the emotions of your characters.

VIVID DESCRIPTIONS

Quote: "...setting is more than a mere backdrop for action; it is an interactive aspect of your fictional world that saturates the story with mood, meaning, and thematic connotations." —*veteran writing instructor, Jessica Morrell*

I strongly recommend that writers briefly describe the setting at the beginning of each new scene or chapter to help the reader get a visual of the location. Also, writers should include a few vital details about the location by lacing the description throughout the dialogue and action to remind the reader where the scene takes place.

This excerpt should help writers get a clear idea on how to write a descriptive scene using the five senses (sensory details), action, dialogue, and Deep POV. And whenever you can describe something, try to see if it can be revised more effectively through the character actions, like in the example below from my paranormal romance novel, IMMORTAL ECLIPSE.

Please study this example…

DEEP POV:

As we finish touring the second wing, Mrs. Pratt finally opens a door to the left and switches on the light, illuminating a quaint bedroom. It's richly furnished and decorated in a startling, opulent blue softened by the flowered wallpaper.

The fireplace is flanked by a duo of overstuffed armchairs. Heavy damask curtains tied open with braided tassels cover the bay window that has a cushioned window seat. The huge bed looks soft and warm. With my gaze lingering on the stack of decorative pillows, I almost trip over my luggage and the boxes already placed beside it. My fingers trace the plush velvet comforter; I'll enjoy reading by the fire or snuggled in the bed on cold winter nights. The huge walk-in closet is, hands-down, the best feature of the room.

"This is the Blue Room. It has a private bathroom," she said.

"The Blue Room, huh? Wonder why they call it that?" A giggle erupts. Mrs. Pratt clucks her tongue, so I flatten my lips to stifle the laughter.

I wouldn't ordinarily choose blue, yet the color seems calming, like an antidote to the strange feelings I've been experiencing since arriving at Summerwind.

She moves to the door. "We thought it would be better if you were close to the staff's quarters in this wing. On the other side of the house, otherwise there'd be no one around to hear you scream in the darkness. At night..." She frowns and looks away.

I stare at her. *As if that doesn't sound ominous.*

***

Could you grasp how the scene from my novel is vivid and inciting? It lures the reader into the scene with a mixture of description, action, dialogue, and "voice."

Now these longer scenes below are both very different. The first is shallow and bland, with too much *telling* and gives readers a weak visual

Please examine these examples…

SHALLOW:

I went into my father's vast bedroom that had been decorated in an historical style, and I <u>saw</u> a gold mirror over the headboard of the really big bed, and then I <u>noticed</u> a black and golden colored comforter. <u>There was</u> some red curtains hung in the windows. The walls were adorned with flowery wallpaper and <u>there were</u> some pictures of our family's home in the Hamptons.

Then I <u>smelled</u> my mother's perfume, but I <u>realized</u> it was just coming from the flowers that were placed in the room. I <u>knew</u> that my mother would have hated all the money wasted on this room. <u>There was</u> an expensive Persian rug bought for my father's new wife for their wedding anniversary on the floor.

I <u>noticed</u> <u>there was</u> a big screen TV on the far wall and it was the only contemporary exclusion to the bedroom's antique furnishings.

That shallow scene is boring, passive, and just states the facts. But this second Deeper POV scene has "voice" and action and stays in close-and-personal.

DEEP POV (sensory details):

Sighing heavily, I hesitated in the doorway of my father's gaudily redecorated suite. I rolled my eyes as I took in the vast bedroom decorated in the style of Louis XVI, with a gilt-framed mirror hanging over the headboard of the king-sized, black-and-gold-upholstered bed.

Is he for real?

I stepped inside, my fingers lightly trailing along the flowered wallpaper, and paused to study the photos of the family's beach house in the Hamptons. At least my father hadn't removed those...

When I turned, my shoulder brushed against the red velvet curtains covering the windows. When the fragrance of lilacs drifted over from the flower arrangement on the dresser, my heart stuttered. The scent reminded me of my dearly departed mother. And she would be turning over in her grave at all the money my father had wasted on this luxurious room.

I shook my head when I caught sight of the Persian rug bought at auction from Sotheby's as a gift to my father's gold-digging third wife for their fifth wedding anniversary.

Glancing upward at the wall, I grunted at the lone modern exception to the room's historical décor—a fifty-inch plasma TV.

***

Now ask yourself: which example caused more impact?

Words and phrases with powerful sensory connotations always increase a writers chances of producing an empathic response. Some things to continuously consider whenever you're revising the setting:

Do the word choices paint vivid images in the reader's mind?

Do the descriptions place the reader in the scene?

Do they make the reader an active participant in the story instead of a mere observer?

It's easy for writers in early drafts to depend on simple, straightforward descriptions of rooms and settings. Using Deep POV does add more words to your scenes, but the experience you'll give your readers will be well worth it.

DRAMATIC SCENES

Quote: "Let your description unfold as a character moves throughout the scene. Consider which details your character would notice immediately, and which might register more slowly. Let your character encounter those details interactively." — *columnist, Moira Allen, editor of Writing World*

Deep POV just means painting a more vivid picture for your readers through your POV character. How they "see" the world and describe it for the readers is what gives a writer their own unique style and the character its "voice."

When writing in Deeper POV, a writer should always include the five senses and other sensory details to make the scene very visual and more *real* for the reader.

Here are two different scenes of a girl walking through a residential neighborhood that were taken from one of my short stories. The first is written in a *telling* style (weak visual). Telling does convey the facts and details, but it does so in a flavorless and nondescript way. (I have underlined what I consider to be shallower writing.)

Please carefully study this longer example…

SHALLOW:

Andrea noticed that Elm Street looked deserted. The residential houses looked very quiet and unoccupied inside. There were no other people around her, and it made her feel uneasy.

She realized the sky was a very white color. Andrea was feeling more anxious as if someone was watching her. She walked quickly down the street and she heard the fallen leaves crunch.

She saw a woman hanging clothes on a line. The woman noticed Andrea walk by and lifted her head. Andrea could smell the scent of laundry. Andrea realized the smell reminded her of her mother.

"Hello," Andrea said timidly.

The woman looked at her and she said coldly, "Good morning."

Andrea saw big truck drive past with a gassy smell from the exhaust. It made her cough. Andrea looked around. She realized that the woman hanging the laundry was gone.

I need to get to Rachel's house, she thought. Before they find out that I left.

She turned around and felt her body collide into a tree. She hurt her arm on a branch. She walked faster until she saw her best friend's house further down the street. Andrea stopped and let out a heavy sigh of relief. Her friend lived near the high school. There was a lot of houses that looked the same.

Andrea heard a car turn the corner at a slow pace, and she suddenly felt scared so she ran to the house. She felt herself trip and fall down. She was feeling apprehensive when she stood up and then she tasted blood because she had bitten her lip.

Suddenly, the driver started to drive very fast toward her.

She got frightened and she ran to the porch, then she knocked on the door. "I need help!" she shouted fearfully.

***

Now please compare the next example revised with Deeper POV. And remember that applying any of the five senses to a scene will deepen the experience for the reader, and in some cases, even induce an emotional response. Also, try to include emotional reactions, internal-dialogue, and physical actions to spice up your descriptions and avoid a boring list of details.

DEEP POV:

Elm Street seemed deserted. The suburban homes appeared strange and silent, like houses in an abandoned ghost town. Andrea hurried down the sidewalk, her dirty sneakers crunching on the crisp autumn leaves. The sky was not cerulean, but milky and opaque, like a giant sink turned upside down.

She slowed her steps, a cold tremor racing up her spine. She glanced over her shoulder for the hundredth time.

Just get to Rachel's house. No one is following you. They don't know that you've escaped...

Her gaze darted left, then right. From someone's backyard, a big dog barked, the noise echoing off the vacant-looking homes. Andrea quickened her pace, shoving her hands into the pockets of her winter coat.

A woman hanging clothes on a line, glanced up as she passed by, and the scent of fresh laundry and fabric softener polluted the air. Andrea smiled. The floral scent brought back memories of helping her mother with the housework.

"Hello," Andrea said with a slight smile.

"Good morning," the plump woman said, her tone cold and un-friendly.

A delivery truck rumbled down the tree-lined street, spewing noxious exhaust. Coughing, Andrea peered behind her again. The street remained empty. But the woman hanging laundry was gone.

Andrea turned so abruptly that her body smacked into a tree. The rough bark of the birch chafed the tender flesh of her arm.

Rubbing the spot, she quickened her steps until the house came into view. The tension in her shoulders slightly diminished. She was safe now. Her best friend only lived two streets away from the high school, but the walk felt like it had taken hours. The cookie-cutter house resembled all the others in the neighborhood, except for the shabby porch swing and the flaking yellow paint.

A car slowly turned the corner, and Andrea's heartbeat ramped up. *They had found her!*

She sprinted toward the house. Tripping on a loose shoelace, she fell forward onto her knees. Shakily, she stood and ran her tongue over her lips, the coppery tang of blood filling her mouth.

The driver hit the gas and the car flew down the street, coming straight at her.

Dashing up the rickety steps, she pounded a fist on the door. "Help me, please!"

***

After reading the second scene, which do you think painted a more vivid picture for the reader?

Incorporating Deeper POV in your fiction writing is a great way of making any scene multi-dimensional.

Here are a few more examples of Deeper POV and how it applies to setting. The shallower sentences are considered *telling* the reader information by writing descriptions in a straightforward manner, which is fine on occasion if needed, but I want to inspire writers to *dig deeper* to make their fictional world as three-dimensional as possible.

Please take a look at these examples…

SHALLOW: I thought the forest looked tall and huge.

DEEP POV: Within the vast forest, the towering trees swayed in the breeze, their spindly branches waving hello.

SHALLOW: He noticed that the room was sparse and it felt cold.

DEEP POV: A chill shivered over his skin. The vacant room seemed lonely and unused.

SHALLOW: There were very tall buildings in this part of the city.

DEEP POV: The soaring buildings with their concrete heads in the clouds cast long shadows on the sidewalks below.

SHALLOW: The hillsides looked enormous and they had dry grass.

DEEP POV: The rolling hills resembled an endless expanse of balding grey heads.

SHALLOW: There was a bad storm coming.

DEEP POV: The horizon lit up with white light followed by the loud grumble of thunder.

SHALLOW: The night looked dark and it had a big moon.

DEEP POV: The darkness fell quickly like a shadowy blanket over the land and moonlight struck the sleeping homes like cold silver.

SHALLOW: There were big homes that looked affluent and expensively furnished in this area.

DEEP POV: The area was dominated by impressive mansions with fluted Corinthian columns on the lower and upper stories.

***

Here is another excerpt taken from my NA series, *Sorority Row* that shows writers how to describe a setting by adding sensory details through Deeper POV.

Please closely examine this "setting" example…

DEEP POV:

My new roommate and I were polar opposites. Her name was Vanessa Carmichael and she apparently guzzled energy drinks by the gallon, and her tousled copper hair looked like the "before" picture in a Pantene commercial. At least she seemed nice and normal. I wouldn't have to worry about her doing anything weird like stealing my underwear or taking cell phone pictures of me while I slept to post on Instagram.

Our shared room was enormous compared to my old dormitory. Stevenson Hall had an ancient brick façade, but they'd remodeled the interior to create larger rooms. Apparently, not all dorm rooms resembled dank prison cells with painted cinder block walls. The rooms were more like an expensive apartment than regular campus housing. Even better, the dorms had single-gender floors.

While Vanessa talked a mile a minute, folded clothes on her bed, and sipped a Red Bull, I inspected her—*incredibly* cluttered—side of the room. I flicked a glance at the red poster with that lame phrase "Keep Calm and Carry On" in white lettering over her headboard. Vanessa had fastened a corkboard to the wall above her desk, pinned with snapshots of her high school debate team and blue ribbon awards for science and math. Piles of Old Navy hoodies and graphic shirts and bell-bottom cords were scattered on her dark green comforter.

***

After reading that last scene, did you notice how I weaved a combination of description, introspection, and "voice" into the narrative?

So instead of just describing something in bland detail, writers should try to lace in some of the five senses, emotional responses, "voice," and action to make the description of a setting even more powerful and visual for their readers.

Please remember as you revise your own work that these are only guidelines and examples meant to help writers develop their own style in crafting dynamic settings and locations.

CHARACTERIZATION

Quote: "Voice is the "secret power" of great writing." —*bestselling author, James Scott Bell*

Using the methods outlined in this chapter will help writers create three-dimensional characters who will come alive within their complex fictional worlds by captivating their readers with deeper layers of characterization.

One of the critical elements to differentiate good writing from just average storytelling relates to how the writer handles the point-of-view. That's why, I strongly feel that Deep POV is tightly connected to *voice,* which is a big part of characterization in my opinion.

In this chapter, I'll try my best to explain "voice" in the terms that I understand them, and clarify how important it is to convey that through Deeper POV.

I consider the phrase "show, don't tell" to primarily specify going deeper into a character's POV. It isn't just stating the facts or information, but giving the reader a glimpse of the world through the senses of the POV character. It allows the reader to become more immersed within the storyline and feel a stronger connection to the character(s).

A lot of manuscripts that I've edited over the years were lacking any "voice." So it is my belief that some writers don't fully comprehend what it means, or how it can deepen the characterization and give your writing a distinctive style.

So let me put it this way...just as everyone has their own characteristic way of speaking or expressing themselves, a writer's characters should also have a distinctive "voice" that clearly comes across in the narrative.

I advise the writers that I work with to strengthen "voice" by using phrasing that reflects the overall tone of their book, along with the POV character's unique personality. How the character reacts or responds in any given situation should be distinctive to their individuality. So choose your nouns and verbs carefully. Being specific about even small details like the weather, description of settings, or objects can create a stronger impression of that character's POV.

These next two longer scenes were each taken from one of my novels, UNDER SUNLESS SKIES. The first one lacks any real emotional descriptions and has no "voice." (I have underlined what I consider to be shallower writing.)

Please carefully compare these examples...

SHALLOW:

I really hate my boring math class. I'm not listening to Mrs. Brooks talk about angles and measurements because I do not care. I will never use this type of math in the real world. I <u>look</u> up at the clock. There is fifteen minutes before the bell rings.

I <u>feel bored and sleepy.</u> I put my elbows on my desktop, and then I put my forehead into my hands and I close my eyes. Mrs. Brooks continues to talk about equations and her loud voice is <u>irritating.</u>

"If Miss Masterson paid attention in class," Mrs. Brooks says, "I wouldn't have to re-explain how the trigonometric ratios are derived from triangle similarity considerations today."

I don't glance up, because I don't want to see her ugly face.

"Are you paying attention, Miss Masterson, or are you in a world of your own again?"

I hear several students laugh. I feel my cheeks heat with embarrassment.

I still do not look up at her unattractive features. "No, I'm not preoccupied," I say sullenly.

"Then would you like to share with the class what you were doing that is more important than listening to my lecture?" Mrs. Brooks asks impatiently.

Now I feel enraged as I lift my head. My classmates laugh, and I hear them move in their seats as they turn to look at me.

***

The revised scene has been revised with Deep POV and it has "voice," tension-soaked dialogue, introspection, and characterization. It is much longer and more detailed, but creates a much more vivid scene in the reader's mind.

Please study this rewritten example…

DEEP POV:

Now I'm trapped sitting in class, not really listening to Mrs. Long-winded Brooks drone on about angles and measurements. I glare at the back of Hayden's head, silently willing him to turn around and acknowledge me. It feels like I'm a minor character being faded out of a TV series, as if I've had one minute of total screen time with Hayden.

Clenching my jaw, every muscle in my body feels taut. I *hate* how he just blew me off. I *hate* that my parents aren't trustworthy. I *hate* Zach and his fat-shaming slurs. I *hate* the mysterious person leaving threats in my locker. And I *hate* this uncomfortable metal desk with gum stuck to the side of it.

The seconds tick by. I glance at the clock hanging on the wall. Thirty-nine tortuous minutes before class ends. I want to be anywhere but here. I almost wish demons would attack the school and drag me to Hell, or worse…somewhere where there's no chocolate. Now that would be pure evil!

Mrs. Brooks lectures on equations and her shrill voice sounds like braying sheep in heat. A sharp throbbing spreads across my forehead. I rest my elbows on the desk, then lower my head into my palms and close my eyes.

"If Miss Masterson would be more attentive…" Mrs. Brooks walks down the aisle, the rubber soles of her cheap pumps squeaking on the floor. "Then I wouldn't have to waste everyone's time by re-explaining how the trigonometric ratios derive from triangle similarity considerations." Her footsteps pause at my desk.

I keep my head down, my eyes squeezed shut. If I lift my head and look at her, I'll be compelled to stare at that mole on her chin. The one with the long, black witch hair sticking out of it.

"Are you paying attention, Miss Masterson?" She taps an impatient foot, then moves further along the aisle. "I do *not* tolerate sleeping in my classroom."

Jeez. Adults think they're *so* superior all the time. Just like my lying-deceiving parents.

"You do know that it's not Halloween, right?" Emma says in a loud whisper, twisting in her seat. "You look like a wannabe vampire in that strange getup."

The sarcastic edge in her voice grates on my last nerve.

With my head still cradled in my hands, I'm feeling the height of bitchiness coming on strong. So my style's dark with a side of edgy? What's the issue?

Slowly, I lift my head and shoot Emma a heated glare. "If you must know, it's Halloween *every* day at my house."

Emma's pink mouth gapes, then snaps shut. Most of my classmates turn in their seats to watch the impending showdown. Several kids even stop scribbling in their notebooks. Hayden hangs his head and shakes it as if in disapproval.

"You call *that* style? More like chubby couture." Emma snickers. "You must've read one too many Anne Rice novels. Unless you're praying you'll never come in contact with direct sunlight."

My cheeks heat, my skin piping so hot it feels as if I've stuck my face in an oven.

Several students giggle. Hayden's shoulders stiffen. Emma smiles and her best friend Kaitlyn rolls her squinty eyes.

I wonder if Emma is the blackmailer. Or maybe it's her evil sidekick, Kaitlyn. Their combined Sloane-hate places them on my *Do Not Trust* list. I size Emma up. She's wearing what might be the most preppy outfit I've ever seen outside an 80's Brat Pack movie, a white button-up shirt under a pink cardigan and capris with plaid flats. She almost looks too innocent to be a suspect, but her bitchiness is singeing through her good girl persona.

"Emma, cut it out," Hayden says under his breath.

Mrs. Brooks crosses both arms over her chest, obviously expecting me to apologize. "Are you quite done disrupting my class, Miss Masterson?"

Usually, I'm incapable of making people feel bad. Even if they're in the process of mocking me. Not today.

"Yeah, can I go back to taking my nap now?" I yawn, then mumble, "As if I'll ever use this stupid math anyway."

"Get out of my classroom!" Mrs. Brooks points an index finger at the door. "Go to the principal's office."

***

Besides all the other key ingredients a writer needs to enhance a scene, "voice" is among the most vital to Deeper POV. Spend some time getting to know your characters. Fill out character interviews and profiles to gain some insight into their temperaments and personalities, and then let that shine through in your narrative by use of the Deep POV technique.

Each character's voice personifies more than their speech or internal-thoughts. The narrative should express it as well. When you write a scene in a certain character's POV, each sentence in that scene has to read as though it is being experienced, felt, and expressed by that character.

One easy way to add "voice" to any character is to incorporate a few personal quirks, or unique phrases, rather than impersonal or formal syntax. Strive to include words meaningful to the character's personality and world views within the storyline.

CHARACTER VOICE

Quote: "Clichéd, superficial characters are the mark of a poor writer. A great character can save an overly simplistic plot, but no amount of action will make up for unbelievable or shallow characters. A good character has the same kind of depth, complexity, and believability as an interesting person." —*author, Magdalena Ball*

Like I mentioned in the last chapter, realistic "voice" is the characteristic speech and thought patterns of your narrator, like a persona. Because voice has so much to do with the reader's experience of a work of literature, it is one of the most important elements in any piece of writing to create three-dimensional characters.

I have included two scenes to show writers the difference between "voice" and bland narration. The first one has shallow writing with lots of *telling* and hardly any "voice" or sensory details. (In the shallow example, I did not underline the obvious areas of shallower writing, but see if you can easily spot it.)

Please carefully compare these examples...

SHALLOW:

Sam Harrington heard the door open and he looked up from his comic book where he worked at the Book Shark. He saw a fat man with brown hair and eyes and a big nose walk into the bookstore. Sam noticed that the man was wearing jeans with socks and sandals and a T-shirt. He watched him walk past the bookcases and then he went toward Sam.

"Can I help you?" Sam asked in curiosity as the man approached.

"Here to pick up my book," he said loudly. "My name is McGrath."

"Sorry, this week's order hasn't come in yet. Do you wanna give us a call next—" Sam started to say but McGrath cut him off, so he stopped talking. (*None of this is needed at the end of the dialogue.*)

McGrath leaned across the counter and Sam thought he looked very angry. "What do you mean my book is not here in the store?" he asked raucously.

Sam opened his mouth to respond but stopped. He was nervous because the man was so furious and Sam didn't know what to do.

McGrath's face looked red and he tried to relax. "Where is my book?" he repeated more calmly.

Now, this second scene has been rewritten to clearly reveal "voice" in the speech, internal-thoughts, and the narrative, and it even shows a Deeper POV.

Please compare this revised example...

DEEP POV:

It was a slow day at the Book Shark. Sam Harrington stood at one end of the bookstore in the self-help section, stuffing last week's shipment of books onto the shelves.

The bell over the door chimed and Sam glanced up. A waft of car exhaust and brewing coffee from the Starbucks next door entered the room as the door creaked opened.

A customer entered the shop and maneuvered around the bookshelves with a heavy limp. When Sam caught a glimpse of the man's clothing, his eyebrows rose. It was the middle of summer and the guy had on jeans with socks and leather Birkenstocks. *Crazy.*

Sam hurried past a pimply teenager sitting on the floor, reading a book and an old lady with blue hair—*well, it looked blue*—scanning the covers of the romance novels on sale.

Sam walked behind the counter and faced the new customer. "Can I help you, sir?"

"Here to pick up my book," the man said in a gruff tone. "Name's McGrath."

"Sorry, this week's order hasn't come in yet. Do you wanna give us a call next—"

"Whaddya mean my book didn't arrive?" The stocky man leaned over the glass counter, and glared at Sam. His dark brown hair fell into his beady hazel eyes, and McGrath pushed the strands aside with a pudgy hand. He lowered his head, and blew out a breath soured by stale beer and cigarettes.

Sam's shoulders slumped. *Great. Another pissed off customer. It's not my fault the shipment is always freaking late.*

McGrath straightened, tugging at the collar of his faded Aerosmith T-shirt as if in an attempt to collect himself. His bulbous nose twitched. "*Now.* Where's my book on ritual human sacrifices, boy?"

* * *

Each example presents the same scenario, but how the character relates it to the reader and the way the scene is *shown* through the words used to convey the character's reactions and views is what reveals "voice." The first one is *telling* the reader in a bland way, but in the second version, we get a glimpse of the character's unique personality through Deeper POV.

"Voice" can add an extra layer of characterization to any novel, and it can avoid making your character seem like the dreaded Mary-Sue type.

Yes, writing with Deeper POV and "voice" often adds more words to your prose, but it is far more interesting and reveals a character's personality aka "voice."

Let's use another example in order to clarify what I mean. Here's a snippet from my science fiction novel, LOST IN STARLIGHT, before revision (no "voice"). The heroine has lost her cell phone and she suspects that the new guy at school has stolen it. (I have underlined what I consider to be shallower writing.)

Please study and compare these examples…

SHALLOW:

The next day, I go past my typical lunch table. I disregard my friends as they watch me I walk across the cafeteria. I am furious with Hayden Lancaster. I had no phone last night and I felt weird without it. This is the first chance I've had all day to talk to him. If I'd known where Hayden lived, I would've gone to his house in anger last night.

How did he take my iPhone? He must have removed the device from my purse while I was talking to Devin, I thought.

Viola sees me walk by, and says silently, *Where are you going?* And I point a finger in Hayden's direction.

I notice sunlight shines through the windows. I smell pizza and I hear the sound of a soda can opening

Hayden is sitting alone with a bowl of pasta. Two drumsticks are near the bag. I'm still so infuriated with him. I see that he is wearing pants and a black shirt.

I set my lunchbox on the table and then sit down. I hear the loud sound it makes and see how it causes people to look at us, but it doesn't bother me.

"Where's my phone?" I ask angrily.

I watch Hayden sit back. "What's up, Emo Chick?" he asks casually.

"Emo? Really?" I say with irritation.

I watch him look at me in my outfit. Why is he staring at me like that? What is wrong with my fashion sense?

"Okay, then, Goth Girl," he says flippantly.

I hate stereotypes, I think to myself.

DEEP POV ("voice" and characterization):

The next day, I bypass my usual table at lunch, ignoring my friends and their curious stares as I storm across the cafeteria, swinging my Monster High lunchbox like a weapon. I have an animalistic urge to destroy Hayden Flippin' Lancaster. Being without my phone all night felt like I was missing an actual limb. I even tried calling my cell, but no one answered.

This is the first chance I've had all day to confront him. If I'd known where Hayden lived, I would've been kicking down his door last night.

I just don't know exactly *how* he managed to steal my iPhone undetected. But he must've snatched it out of my purse when my back was turned while I was talking to Devin in the hallway. I should've expected this when I stupidly blabbed about filming his epic dog rescue.

Viola watches me march past, mouthing: *Where are you going?* And I stab a finger in Hayden's direction.

Super Boy thinks he's so smart. *Well, he's just met his Kryptonite!*

Sunlight trickles through the windows, dancing over the tables and the tacky orange chairs. The nauseating odor of greasy pizza wafts from the kitchen area, and the hiss of a soda can opening resonates throughout the crowded space.

Hayden's sitting alone with his sack lunch and a plastic bowl of pasta. Two grungy drumsticks rest against the bag. Guess where I'd like to stick those. I try not to think about how hot he looks in urban decayed pants and a black V-neck shirt. He might be the silent, stoic type of man candy, but I'm about to crack his tough guy shell.

I drop my lunchbox on the table with a *bang* and slide onto an empty seat. The clatter draws attention, but I don't care about making a scene.

"Where's my phone?" I demand.

Hayden nonchalantly leans back and crosses his legs in that dude-*esque*, one ankle-over-the-opposite-thigh. "What's up, Emo Chick?"

"Emo? Really?"

He checks me out from head-to-toe in my aquamarine dress with a white skull pattern, black knee-high socks, and riding boots. My cute Rock Rebel studded chain purse rests on one shoulder, and my hair is styled in a high ponytail. I am *so* looking glam-rock today!

"Okay, then, Goth Girl."

Even worse.

* * *

Now one last piece of advice, I think even secondary characters should have a distinct personality that separates them from other characters.

The subsequent excerpt is taken from my new adult romance novel, SMASH INTO YOU, and it shows how even a secondary character has her own personality. Vanessa (the secondary character) has a very unique voice, as well as my spunky narrator.

Please closely examine this example with "voice" for both characters...

DEEP POV:

"...then I laughed so hard, I nearly peed in my hemp underwear...*Hello?* Are you even listening to me?"

I glanced up. "Oh. Yeah. Sorry. What were you saying?"

Vanessa pushed up her glasses. "You don't care that I took the right side? Because I like being closer to the window and you came a day late—"

"It's fine," I said, shifting on my bed and lowering the novel I'd been reading.

My new home. This square, off-white room with its squeaky wooden floor only had two closets that barely fit all my clothes and shoes. My gaze swept over my side of the room, which resembled an ad from an IKEA catalog, decorated in girly pastel colors of turquoise, white, and pink, with two prints of Vincent van Gogh's artwork gracing the walls. Over my headboard, I'd hung a string of twinkle lights.

I fluffed the row of pillows behind my head and stretched out my legs. I'd loved shopping for all my new stuff. My dad just handed over his credit card with a warning not to go *too* crazy. It allowed me to imagine a completely different life to go with my brand-new persona.

"If it's gonna be an issue, I can move my stuff," Vanessa said.

"I don't care. Honest."

Vanessa took a swig of her drink. She blinked her big owlish eyes behind square-framed glasses. "Awesome. My roommate last year was *sooo* picky. She was always borrowing my stuff without asking, and making out with her emo boyfriend…"

Chatty Vanessa would be my cellmate for the next year. *Oh, yay.* I already wanted to duct tape her mouth shut.

* * *

This additional chapter on "voice" should help writers to really understand how to depict a character's distinctive personality within the narrative.

FIRST-PERSON POV

Quote: "Emotions are critical to making a character feel *real*, but describing them from afar can sometimes leave a reader feeling a little disconnected from that character. The descriptions don't feel like a character feeling, but like the author *telling* the reader how the character feels." —*author and blogger, Janice Hardy*

As requested by a number of writers, I have included a chapter on writing Deep POV through the eyes and ears and senses of a first-person narrator.

When you're writing in first-person point-of-view always strive to stay in Deeper POV. Actually, most editors and bestselling authors would agree that first-person narratives are the easiest way to avoid *telling*.

While writing in deep first-person POV, try to make sure that each scene is intimate and detailed for your readers by being specific whenever possible and revising any filter words.

Even with first-person POV, you're never limited in describing a character's facial expressions or emotions. Although, the first-person narrator can't see his or her own face, a writer can still vividly describe the character's expressions and emotions and body language.

There are many ways to "show" reactions or emotions for a first-person POV narrator, instead of just *telling* the reader what the character's emotions are directly. Writers should revise any shallow words like "felt / feel" to describe an emotion.

Please compare these examples…

SHALLOW: Staring into the utter darkness, I felt my palms grow damp.

DEEP POV: Staring into the utter darkness, my palms grew damp.

SHALLOW: I felt my face get hot in embarrassment.

DEEP POV: My cheeks burned at his rude remark.

SHALLOW: I felt sweaty and nervous before the talent audition.

DEEP POV: Sweat beaded my forehead and I restlessly paced backstage.

SHALLOW: I felt sad on my long walk home.

DEEP POV: My lips pulled downward at the corners and I blinked back tears while I drudged home.

SHALLOW: I felt really angry at Amy for forgetting my birthday again.

DEEP POV: I stomped my foot. "Seriously, Amy? You forgot my birthday day *again*?"

SHALLOW: I felt lust fill my body when I saw Kenneth.

DEEP POV: A burst of sizzling desire heated my body as Kenneth entered the room.

***

I mainly write in first-person and that's why most of the excerpts are taken from my own work as examples of Deeper POV.

Here is another one with too many filtering references…

SHALLOW:

I could not see in the darkness as I moved through the brambles.

This is really creepy, I thought.

There was an old farmhouse somewhere near Maple Drive. I thought I would be okay if I could just find the path. Suddenly, I saw headlights, blinding me. Then I heard a car on the road and I felt my body freeze. My legs felt wobbly and I knew my breathing had increased. I heard the car rev its engine and it sounded scary.

I knew I had to move out of the way when I noticed the old car drive past.

Here is the scene revised without the filter words…

DEEP POV:

I stumbled in the darkness through the brambles.

This is really creepy.

An old farmhouse sat somewhere near Maple Drive. I'd be okay if I could just find the path. Suddenly, headlights shone in my eyes, blinding me. The crunch of tires on the gravel road caused me to freeze in my tracks. My legs wobbled and my breathing sped up. The car revs its engine ominously.

I leaped out of the way just as the rusty Buick rumbled past.

***

Since I primarily write in first-person POV, I don't think it's necessarily incorrect for my characters to "interpret" the expressions or body language of another character as long as they aren't too specific.

This next excerpt is from, LOST in STARLIGHT, which will show writers how to lace "voice" with action and humor into your first-person descriptions. This example shows embarrassment (along with other emotions) without stating the feeling.

Please study this first-person POV scene...

DEEP POV:

"It's just..." His voice is soft. "I want to be clear, we can't be anything more than friends, Sloane...you'll only end up collateral damage."

I frown. "Collateral damage? What the hell does that even mean?"

Hayden takes a shallow breath. "Dammit, I'm saying this all wrong."

"Ya think?"

"It's to protect you."

I arch an eyebrow. "From?"

"I can't..." He groans and his long bangs flop onto his forehead, nearly obscuring his anxious stare. "I want you to be safe and I can be really impulsive. It's just that when I catch the way you look at me sometimes, I get the feeling you'd like something more than friendship."

Oh. My. God.

Am I that obvious?

An even hotter flush steals across my face and sweeps down my neck. I am beyond mortified. This is bad. So bad. I need to take my fragile, wounded ego and go hide. For, oh…like a decade.

For a moment, my vision goes black and red. My body shudders. I need to get away from him. *Now.* I step stiffly forward and trip on my shoelace, staggering off the curb and onto the pavement…

***

Here are more examples of writing Deeper POV from the first-person perspective. Please carefully compare these examples…

SHALLOW: I felt light-headed and I wanted to throw up.

DEEP POV: A bout of nausea struck my senses and my body swayed.

SHALLOW: I was scared of the dark and I forgot my flashlight.

DEEP POV: My heart rate kicked into overdrive. The light switch didn't work, and I had stupidly forgotten to bring a flashlight.

SHALLOW: I was shocked to discover that I won the contest.

DEEP POV: The breath caught in my lungs. *I'd won the contest!*

SHALLOW: I became thoughtful. "Tell me more," I inquired.

DEEP POV: I frowned, tapping a finger on my chin. "Tell me more."

SHALLOW: My face had a <u>panicked look</u> on it.

DEEP POV: Every molecule in my body turned icy, and my expression froze.

SHALLOW: I'm <u>really worried</u> about Karen's illness.

DEEP POV: My palms are sweating. The doctors just *had* to find a way to save Karen.

SHALLOW: I knew my face was <u>pinched in disgust.</u> (Cliché)

DEEP POV: My lips turned downward and I turned away.

SHALLOW: I <u>heard</u> Janice running up the driveway.

DEEP POV: Janice's sneakered feet pounded the gravel on the driveway.

SHALLOW: I <u>saw</u> Hank stealing a candy bar.

DEEP POV: Out of the corner of my eye, I caught Hank stuffing a candy bar into his pocket.

SHALLOW: "You are a liar," I said, my <u>facial expression turning into a scowl.</u>

DEEP POV: "You're such a liar!" I said, rolling my eyes.

***

Could you grasp how removing filtering references can instantly deepen the POV?

Here is an excerpt taken from the first chapter of my young adult paranormal romance novel, BEAUTIFULLY BROKEN, (free to download or read on wattpad for a limited time) to give writers another example on how to cleverly write Deeper POV from a first-person narrator. The character becomes nervous and frightened when she suspects that she's not alone in her bedroom, but the emotions are never blatantly stated in this short scene.

Please carefully examine this example...

DEEP POV:

For as long as I could remember, I'd heard whispers in the shadows. Black, twisting shapes that chilled my blood. Slithering through the night, their greenish skin, crimson eyes, and sharp claws were illuminated even in the dark.

Sunlight often meant the difference between life and death.

I normally felt safe during the day, with the heat of the sun brushing my skin, so that morning, when the shadows showed up in my bedroom, I barely recognized their eerie whispering.

The desk lamp flickered, startling me. I stared at the last line I'd typed on my essay for English class, one hand hovering over the keyboard.

Homework could wait.

I raised my head and closed the laptop. My heart hammered. A hint of chilling menace climbed up my spine. Finishing homework was the last thing on my mind.

The spooky, inhuman whispering grew more intense.

Setting the laptop aside, I jumped off the bed, nearly tripping over my long nightgown. I scanned the dark bends and edges of the room. The swirling azure colors of the witch-ball suspended over the bed rotated in a slow circle. I got down on my hands and knees to check under the bed. Nothing.

The closet door was open a crack. I stood up and wavered, shoulders hitching.

I hesitated for a second before walking over to the closet and kicking the door open. On tiptoes, I leaned over the threshold, stretching to grasp the brass chain, and then gave it a yank. Light bled across dirty laundry, illuminating metal hangers scattered on the floor. Dusty board games littered the shelf, and haphazardly hanging clothes swayed on the bar. My fuzzy bunny slippers stared upward with glassy button eyes. Nothing unusual.

So why was I so freaked?

The feeling, indistinct but ominous, lingered like the remnants of a bad dream. I couldn't isolate the source. But something felt *wrong*.

The closet light and lamp blew out. As I turned around, my peripheral vision caught a maelstrom of shadows. Things withered within it. Something snaked past my leg....

***

There is one rhetorical question in this scene, but besides that, it stays in a very tight and close viewpoint.

Now I challenge you to rewrite a scene in your own story and use Deep POV to get inside the head of your first-person narrator and keep your readers in close-and-personal.

One last word of advice, the first-person narrator can *only* reveal his/her own thoughts and feelings and reactions, and then merely assume or guess the responses or meanings of facial expressions of the other characters. A first-person character is <u>not</u> a mind-reader, so be careful of this POV violation.

The next few chapters will cover on how to revise "stating a feeling or reaction" instead of *telling* the reader what the character is feeling. All of the Deep POV examples in this handbook have already been used in my published novels or short stories, so you'll need to come up with your own unique variations.

CHARACTER DESCRIPTIONS

Quote: "The characters in our stories, songs, poems, and essays embody our writing. They are our words made flesh. Sometimes they even speak for us, carrying much of the burden of plot, theme, mood, idea, and emotion. But they do not exist until we describe them on the page. Until we anchor them with words, they drift, bodiless and ethereal. They weigh nothing; they have no voice."— *excerpt from "Word Painting" by Rebecca McClanahan*

This chapter focuses on ways that writers can describe a character's physical appearance though Deep POV. (Some of these topics are also covered in my handbook, *"Craft Vivid Scenes and Dynamic Characters,"* but I have expanded some of that information in this guide.)

Character descriptions can be tough to write and so many writers neglect to add physical descriptions to the narrative. When we describe a character's physical appearance, sometimes precise facts about their features, or height and weight, are not quite visual enough.

How you ever read a book and visualized the main character as a lanky, brown-haired nerd, only to discover fifty pages into the story that the character was a brawny, tan, blond guy?

And if writers use clichéd, colorless descriptions they can be too generic, and they don't really help the reader get a clear image of the characters. Writers should describe the characters as early as possible in a manuscript, but avoid creating a boring list of attributes by using weaker descriptive words. Now, I know some of you will argue that other published writers do this, but most professional editors will consider this to be lazy writing. So avoid using descriptors that simply label a character, *short, fat, young, old,* or *ordinary,* which do not create a clear image.

Readers need vibrant images and physical details to envision fictional characters. So I suggest thoughtfully selecting only those descriptors that evoke the clearest, most revealing impressions. Also, writers should allow their descriptions to multitask to also reveal (*show* rather than *tell*) more about a character's personality and background.

Please take a look at these examples...

SHALLOW:

John was slender and he had very long legs. He had messy brown colored hair. John's lips looked really thin. He usually wore baggy clothes and a baseball cap. He hated to go to work meetings. His boss gave him a dirty look when he yawned at one of the meetings.

DEEP POV:

Man, I hate these boring sale's meetings.

John stretched his long legs under the table and loudly yawned.

When the boss paused in his speech and glared at him, John immediately straightened in his seat and tugged at the drooping waistband of his pants.

Once the meeting concluded, he darted back to his desk. John slouched in his chair, running his slender fingers through his tousled brown hair, and then flipping a baseball cap backwards on his head. He caught sight of his reflection in the laptop monitor and wiped a smudge of mustard from the corner of his thin lips.

***

A clever writer applying the Deep POV method can learn to skillfully tuck the physical characteristics into the narrative by lacing it through action and dialogue. Writers need to make all characters as three-dimensional as possible, so that the reader sees them as real people.

If writers can describe what the character(s) look like, how they feel, and how they react to situations and events unfolding around them, it will make the writing much more powerful.

The best technique is to present just enough relevant details to help your reader instantly "see" the character without doing an info-dump, because the right blend of description, dialogue, and introspection, along with some action can create a stronger image for the reader.

Telling descriptions create weak illustrations that can leave the reader grappling for a visual and feeling disconnected from the characters and the scene.

I have included some examples on how to describe physical characteristics to show you what I mean.

Please take a look at these examples…

SHALLOW:

Cole wore tan pants, and leaned against a car. He had blond hair and blue eyes. His full lips grinned at me. I really liked him.

DEEP POV:

Cole stuffed his hands into the pockets of his wrinkled khakis, reclining his large frame against a shiny black Mustang. The breeze ruffled his blond hair, and I yearned to brush the gold strands out of his cerulean eyes. When those generous lips tipped into an arrogant grin, I knew my heart was in big trouble.

***

These next two scenes are longer, and the first is a bland example with intrusive dialogue tags and wordy sentences. (In the shallow example, I did not underline all the obvious areas of shallower writing, but see if you can easily spot it now that you're more aware of *showing* vs. *telling*.)

Please study and compare these examples…

SHALLOW:

Tad noticed a tall woman in a skirt with bare legs and high-heels enter through the front doors of the building. She had green eyes. He saw that the woman was clutching the handle of a purse very tightly as she examined the lobby. He watched her lick her lips, and then she frowned. She had medium-length blond hair. He noticed that she was wearing an ivory shirt, and there was some blood on the sleeve. He watched as her eyes looked back at the parking lot.

Then she saw the security desk and she walked across the floor toward Tad. He felt nervous, so he sat up before she made it to the desk.

"May I help you, miss?" he asked politely.

She placed her hand on the top of the desktop. He looked down and he saw that she had long red fingernails. Her eyes looked into his, and Tad felt very nervous.

"Can you please tell me what floor I can find Stanley Martin's office?" she asked coldly.

This second scene has been rewritten with "voice" and sensory details.

DEEP POV:

A tall woman wearing a striped skirt, with the longest, smoothest legs, Tad had ever seen entered the building. Her icy blue gaze searched the lobby, her hands clutching the handle of her Fendi purse. She licked her red lips, the corners of her mouth tipping downward. She half turned, staring at the parking lot through the sliding glass doors, before muttering a curse. When she pivoted back around, her silk blouse became partially untucked.

Spotting the security desk, she glided forward, her flaxen hair styled in a feathery bob that bounced off her slim shoulders. Her stilettos clacking against the marble floor echoed like a shotgun going off in the quiet room.

Tad sat up, quickly adjusting his wrinkled uniform and straightening his tie. A waft of her exotic perfume reached Tad before she did.

Damn, she's even sexier up close.

He gave her a toothy grin. "May I help you, miss?"

She studied him for a long second, one long ruby fingernail tapping the polished surface of the desktop. A splatter of blood stained her ivory cuff.

"Can you please tell me what floor I can find Stanley Martin's office?" Her voice was low and cold. The woman withdrew a 38. Special from her purse and pointed the gun at him. "And don't make me use this."

***

These three excerpts were taken from my novel, IMMORTAL ECLIPSE. They both illustrate how writers can describe a character through Deeper POV and "voice" and emotional reactions.

Please closely examine this example...

DEEP POV:

I blink several times at the dark-haired man standing in the doorway, trying not to stare at his eyes, an intense shade of blue. Damn, he was better looking than most male fashion models I've photographed. Mr. Tall, Dark, and Yummy tilts his head as his eyes lock on mine. Even from a distance, I can tell he'll tower over me, and I'm no midget. He's even dressed similar to the man in the portrait: a soft, white linen shirt—bulging biceps stretching the fabric —under a black vest paired with snug pants and chunky boots. Although, he appears to be only in his late twenties, he looks reserved and intimidating.

Conclusion: no sense of style, but still smoking hot.

Please closely examine this next example...

DEEP POV:

Compared to the décor in Pauletta's posh office, the furniture is frayed and outdated, with a stack of law books dusting the desk. The room overlooks the Bay Bridge and smells of day-old cigar. *Yuck.*

Matthew Rosenberg glances up, surprising me with how much he's aged. His wrinkled skin—probably from all those afternoons spent negotiating cases on the golf course—with teeth that flash yellow when he smiles, and pants drooping beneath a gut that strains his shirt buttons. The years spent in California have added bloat and wrinkles that accentuate his every flaw.

Please closely examine this third example...

DEEP POV:

Behind her glass-top desk, Pauletta sits in a sleek black leather chair, which reclines to an almost obscene angle as she crosses her smooth brown legs. She's wearing a silk Hermès scarf draped over a gray blouse, a matching rayon skirt, and *really* cute pair of Bettye Muller heels.

***

Now describing a first-person narrator is a bit trickier, but not impossible if you have the tools and know how.

This next passage was taken from MOONLIGHT MAYHEM in my young adult series, and it should give you a pretty good idea on how to describe a first-person narrator.

Please closely examine this example…

DEEP POV:

I flicked my gaze to Ariana. She stared out the window, her expression pensive. I reached over and gave her hand a squeeze. Glimpsing my skin next to hers reminded me that Ariana and I were total opposites, like sunny skies versus somber clouds. An optimist compared to a pessimist. And not only in personality, but in looks, too. She had blond ringlets, winter pale skin that had a sparkly glow in direct sunlight, and a curvaceous figure.

Me? Well, I'd inherited unusual looking features due to my Sioux lineage on my father's side: an athletic body, high cheekbones, olive complexion, bronze eyes, and thick hair the color of midnight. Yup, she was light to my dark. Even in how we viewed the world.

These next two excerpts were also taken from my novel, MOON-LIGHT MAYHEM, to give writers an idea on how to describe a character's hair.

Please carefully examine these two examples…

DEEP POV:

My ex stood at the counter with his friend and ordered a pizza. His hair tapered in the back and across both sides, but left heavy on top was styled into a spiky mess.

DEEP POV:

Every time I caught sight of my reflection and my unevenly cut, shoulder-length black hair, it reminded me of the wickedness that my crazed mother was capable of doing. Last month, she'd hacked off my long, straight hair in an attempt to break me. It hadn't worked. She'd done other things—*awful things*—which I would never understand. Chopping off my hair had only been one of them. And I hated how it looked now. Taking the scissors, I trimmed the ends so they looked more even and rested on my shoulders. Much better.

***

Here are a few more examples of shallow sentences that "tell" the reader the physical characteristics instead of *showing*. I realize that using Deep POV in descriptions can make the prose wordy, and just *telling* the reader might be a quicker way to reveal a character's personality or describe their looks, but it always creates a weaker visual.

Please take a look at these examples…

SHALLOW: Charles was a fat man who couldn't fit his bulky body onto the lawn chair. His pants ripped in the back when he sat down and his huge belly hung over his pants.

DEEP POV: Charles' cheeks burned red as he squeezed himself down into the lawn chair. *Rippp!* His polyester golf pants split up the back, and his bulging stomach hung over the waistband.

***

Below is an excerpt from one of my novels, SHATTERED SI-LENCE to illustrate how to describe a character's clothing and personality.

Please closely examine this example...

DEEP POV:

Trent shrugged off a worn leather jacket and draped it over an armchair, displaying a long-sleeved black shirt. The guy was the epitome of hip. With artfully mussed hair, low-slung jeans, motorcycle boots, and model good looks, just a glimpse of Trent Donovan caused female hormones to rage, teenage girls to swoon, and mouths to drool.

***

Here's another character description taken from my Sci-Fi romance, LOST IN STARLIGHT. Please closely examine this example...

DEEP POV:

Hayden turns his head and his light brown fauxhawk falls over his forehead in a messy yet somehow deliberate way, landing over his once strikingly blue eye. The other one is green. Besides the rare heterochromia iridis, he seems to be just another smokin' hot brainiac.

I add to my notes: *Weird eye color and member of the Amazing Hair Club.* Check.

***

Don't forget to describe your characters by weaving in descriptions of clothing, age, hair and eye color, height, weight, visible scars, and even nationality, etc. into the scene. Writers should do it by lacing the physical characteristics throughout the action and dialogue.

Adding descriptions of hair may seem silly to some of you, but if you write young adult novels, it will add an extra layer of depth and realism to your storyline.

If a writer learns to sprinkle physical characteristics into a scene mixed with the action, dialogue, and introspection, it will enhance the storyline and enrich the reader's experience. And I strongly suggest that each time a new character is introduced to the storyline, that the writer provides the reader with a visual illustration. Now, it doesn't have to be a lengthy description of the character, a few well-placed descriptive words or action tags should be enough.

FACIAL EXPRESSIONS

Quote: "One of the most difficult problems plaguing writers is how to describe facial expressions. The problem arises if the writer does not describe facial expressions at all, or if they provide cliché, or overused descriptions..." —*freelance writer and English teacher, Roger Colby*

Expressions are one of the universal languages of emotion, because just a *look* can instantly convey whatever a person might be feeling, such as joy, sorrow, anger, or fear, etc. And how your POV characters interprets these expressions is essential to page-turning prose. But for some writers it can be hard to find the right verbs or adjectives to describe facial expressions or emotional reactions, so use this chapter as a handy resource for ideas on describing the expressions of the characters, without *stating the emotion.*

In my opinion, using the filter word: *felt* or *feel* is the weakest way to depict an emotion. If a writer uses shallower writing like, *he felt miserable* or *she felt livid,* or *he was traumatized* or *she was excited* it takes the narrative out of Deeper POV. As writers, we should always be exploring new ways to describe character emotions and expressions.

One way to avoid shallower writing is to express a character's moods, responses, and emotions by describing their reactions and body language. There are endless creative ways to describe expressions and elicit a reader response.

Please take a look at these examples of facial expressions...

Suspicion: Eyes hooded or narrowed

Surprise/shock: Eyes wide or open

Fear/sorrow/disappointment: Lip quivering

Disgust/abhorrence: Nose wrinkles or lips turn downward

Thoughtful/confused: Brow furrows or lips puckered

Sadness/shock: Tears or shaky movements

Annoyed/frustrated: Eye twitching or eye rolling

Inquisitive/doubtful: Raised eyebrow or long stare

Hesitant/uncertain: Biting lips or tugging on ear

Rage/displeasure: Pursed lips or flushed face/ears

Calm/happy: Smiling /body relaxed

***

When describing facial expressions, one thing that a writer can mention is the character's eyes. Eyes are very expressive, and they can tell a reader a lot about what a character is thinking, feeling, or trying to communicate. Eyes that dart around usually indicate a character that is lying or nervous. If a character is lying, then show the reader a slight twitch at the corner of the mouth. The character might avoid eye contact too, if he/she is trying to hide something. Eyes that are big and round can convey surprise. Or eyes that are droopy or lowered can indicate sleepiness or boredom. (But please don't over use "eyes" to convey emotions.)

A writer can also describe a character's mouth to reveal emotions or even a strong reaction. If the character is grinning, it shows that he /she is feeling joyful, content, or satisfied. Sometimes, a character might be hiding a negative or painful emotion behind the mask of a smile. A slight twitch of the upper lip may indicate amusement, or even disgust. When a character is frowning it shows the reader that he/she is unhappy, angry, or even thoughtful. Or if the lips are pulled downward, it could show annoyance.

Writers can show a melancholy expression with tear-filled eyes, slumped posture, drooping mouth, and loud sighs. Or a flushed face with tense shoulders and flashing eyes indicates an angry character.

Please review this list of common facial expressions…

ANGER: Eyebrows squeezed together, brows knitted, eyes squinty, pupils flared, lowered head, nostrils flared, looking upward through a scrunched brow, tight facial muscles, flat lips, flaring nostrils, or an penetrating gaze.

CONTEMPT: Squinty eyes, mouth snapped shut, mouth set in a hard line, or lips pressed together, grinding teeth, muscle in jaw twitching, face turns crimson, ears red or hot, or hardened expression.

EXCITEMENT: Smile shows teeth, eyes wide, flushed cheeks, eyebrows high, twinkle in eyes, tears in eyes, dimples showing, or raised eyebrows.

FEAR: Pale skin, eyebrows are drawn together, trembling mouth, brows furrowed, creased forehead, eyes wide and huge, blinking rapidly, mouth opening and closing, or tense, white lips.

FRUSTRATION: Slanting eyebrows, jaw tightened, face reddened, chin raised, deep frowning, gnashed teeth, tense eyebrows, squinty eyes, lips pulled back, or mouth twisted to one side.

REVULSION: Frowning, gritted teeth, lips drew back in a snarl, lowered head, tense lips, eyebrows drawn together, wrinkled forehead, or pursed lips.

SURPRISE: Wide eyes, mouth hanging open, huge smile, flushed face, gaping, raised eyebrows, pupils are huge, and head held back, intense gaze, and eyebrows raised.

SADNESS: Pale face, lower lip quivered, tears shimmered in eyes, frowning of lips, head hangs low, pouty expression, or gaze downcast.

HAPPINESS: Smiling big with teeth visible, flushed cheeks, crinkle at corners of the eyes, the corners of mouth turned upward, eyes lit up, tears shone in eyes, face glowing.

***

Another great way to describe a character's expression is to avoid using an "external camera" to catalogue facial expressions or body language as an impartial description. Writers should *dig deeper* to show the emotions because these are indications that readers can use to determine how a characters feels or reacts. Sometimes a more complex description of someone's posture, expression, or mannerisms is needed, and on occasion, it's better to just simplify the description by *telling*.

REDUNDANT PHRASES

Quote: "Writers need good descriptions of facial expressions in their stories to help the readers picture the characters, to convey emotions, and to set up lines of dialogue without having to write "said" or any of its synonyms. However, it's easy for us to rely on the same descriptions over and over again." —*author, Bryn Donovan*

A redundant phrase is one used repeatedly to describe an expression, gesture, or emotion.

Please keep in mind that clichés are the enemy of good writing.

I strongly advise the writers that I work with to avoid describing facial expressions by using overworked clichés. If writers resort to using clichés, like *His smile was dazzling* or *Her eyes shone like diamonds* or *His face was red as a beet*, readers will understand the meaning, but the phrases are so unoriginal that it won't have much impact.

By using a stale cliché or redundant phrase, a writer is actually telling the reader that they lack originality. So I encourage writers to craft a more unique description, rather than relying on a cliché.

In this chapter, I have provided helpful alternatives to overused gestures and facial expressions (not saying mine are terribly original) that should inspire writers to describe a gesture, action, or expression in a different way.

I have put together a list of ways to rewrite certain redundant phrases and clichés...

Alternatives for nodded / bobbed head in agreement:

SHALLOW: Spike nodded his head. "That is what I am talking about."

DEEP POV: Spike punched me in the shoulder. "Yeah, man, that's what I'm talking about!"

SHALLOW: He bobbed his head in agreement. (cliché)

DEEP POV: "Uh-huh," he said, his head bobbing like a yo-yo. "Go on."

SHALLOW: Denise gave him a nod. "Yes, I want to go skating."

DEEP POV: "Hell, yeah." Denise's head bounced up and down like a basketball. "I'd love to go roller skating this weekend!"

SHALLOW: Her head nodded. "Yes, I agree."

DEEP POV: Her head fell back, and then her chin tipped downward in quick, jerky movements like a puppet. "Yeah, that sounds good."

SHALLOW: The man agreed and said that he wanted to do it.

DEEP POV: The man put his hands flat on table. "Let's do this!"

Alternatives for smiled:

SHALLOW: He smiled, looking pleased.

DEEP POV: His mouth curved upward, the outer corners of his eyes crinkling.

SHALLOW: She wore a big smile.

DEEP POV: Her mouth widened, the corners lifting heavenward.

SHALLOW: Betty grinned at me. "I would like to go to the dance."

DEEP POV: Betty's lips stretched sideways. "I can't wait to go to the dance."

SHALLOW: Maxine looked happy and she was smiling because Charles wanted to marry her.

DEEP POV: Maxine floated into work. Finally, Charles had asked her to marry him.

SHALLOW: He had a quick grin that made the attraction more intense.

DEEP POV: His lightening grin made my insides turn into mush.

SHALLOW: I liked Sammy's grin, but it upset my calm demeanor.

DEEP POV: Sammy's grin was irresistibly devastating to my calm reserve.

Alternative examples for laughed:

SHALLOW: The villain had an wicked laugh and he glared at the hero, and then told him that he couldn't stop his evil plans.

DEEP POV: His head fell back and acerbic laughter spewed from his lips. "*Muahahaha!* Even you can't stop me, Marvelous Man."

SHALLOW: Sharon laughed hard and bent over at the waist.

DEEP POV: Sharon doubled over, bursts of breathy vowel sounds escaping her mouth. "Heh-heh. Ha-ha…Stop you're killing me."

SHALLOW: Craig chuckled rowdily and then asked if I was serious.

DEEP POV: Craig slapped his knee, hooting loudly. "Are you serious, man?"

SHALLOW: I saw her expression shift into a humorous one.

DEEP POV: A flash of humor crossed her face.

SHALLOW: Dyson had a loud laugh and his eyes were laughing now, too.

DEEP POV: Dyson chortled, and the teasing laughter was back in his eyes.

SHALLOW: Jeanie was giggling and tried to hide her mouth by lifting her hand and covering her mouth to stop the laughter. (*too wordy*)

DEEP POV: Jeanie tittered, covering her mouth with a slim hand.

Alternative examples for shake / shook head:

SHALLOW: Bo did not agree and she shook her head. "Be quiet."

DEEP POV: Bo wagged her blond head. "Shut up."

SHALLOW: She shook her head vehemently. (*cliché*)

DEEP POV: Her dark head swung from side to side like a tennis ball. "*No!* Please, don't hurt Jimmy."

SHALLOW: The woman shook her head and told him about the voices.

DEEP POV: Her head moved left, then right several times before she blurted, "The voices are telling me to steal your car...*and* your wallet."

SHALLOW: She kept shaking her head.

DEEP POV: Pushing the glasses up the bridge of her nose, she said, "I don't see your point."

SHALLOW: Kenzi shook her head in disbelief. (*cliché*)

DEEP POV: Kenzi's eyebrows rose. "Am I supposed to believe you?"

SHALLOW: He was shaking his head.

DEEP POV: He narrowed his eyes and frowned.

SHALLOW: She shook her head in denial. (*cliché*)

DEEP POV: Looking down, her face turned away. "How could this have happened?"

SHALLOW: With a slight shake of her head, she said incredulity, "I do not understand."

DEEP POV: She slightly rubbed her nose. "I need a minute to absorb this info..."

SHALLOW: Eric did not agree with the suggestion and shook his head.

DEEP POV: Eric leaned back further in his throne-like chair. "Are you for real?"

Alternatives for "made a face" / grimace:

SHALLOW: Winifred made a face at me and then showed me that she was going to punch me in the face, and then she told me that she was going to hurt me. (*too wordy and telling*)

DEEP POV: Winifred ground her knuckles into her cheek, squishing one side of her face. "*This* is what's gonna happen to you—if you're not real careful!"

SHALLOW: She made a face of disgust. (*cliché*)

DEEP POV: Her face twisted in ugly, savage glee.

SHALLOW: Sandra was mad and scowled at Tommy White.

DEEP POV: Sandra stuck out her tongue and squashed her eyes. Then she stomped on Tommy White's foot.

SHALLOW: She stared at me with hatred in her eyes. (*cliché*)

DEEP POV: Her head tilted to one side and her eyes narrowed as if I was a bug that needed to be squashed. And squashed *quickly*.

SHALLOW: Sookie wore a scowl on her face.

DEEP POV: Sookie narrowed her eyes before turning away.

SHALLOW: She felt disgusted with me and scowled in my direction.

DEEP POV: She wrinkled her nose and sneered.

Alternatives for shrugged shoulders:

SHALLOW: Tara felt unsure and shrugged her shoulders in dismay.

DEEP POV: Rubbing around her ear, Tara said, "Well, I don't know."

SHALLOW: Jodi shrugged her shoulders. (*What else can a person shrug?*)

DEEP POV: Jodi lifted her shoulder blades, then let them drop. "I don't *why* I stabbed Kenny—I just did."

SHALLOW: He gave off a shrug and told me whatever and that it wasn't a problem.

DEEP POV: He raised and lowered his shoulders. "Whatever. Not my problem, Liz."

SHALLOW: Ryan was shrugging as he told the police he was innocent.

DEEP POV: Ryan's right shoulder rose and fell, his palms upraised. "You can't bust me. I gotta an alibi."

SHALLOW: She gave him a dismissive shrug. (Cliché)

DEEP POV: Her eyes rolled upward. "Whatever."

Alternatives for frowning:

SHALLOW: Stefan deeply frowned. (Cliché)

DEEP POV: Stefan's face flushed, puffing out his cheeks.

SHALLOW: Lend was frowning at me and I became nervous.

DEEP POV: The muscles in his forehead were constricting, and I knew Lend well enough to know that this was when he was most dangerous.

SHALLOW: He frowned and looked confused.

DEEP POV: "That doesn't make sense..." His lips flattened together. "The magic spell should've worked."

SHALLOW: My boss looks angry and he's wearing a frown.

DEEP POV: His bushy brows squeeze together, and he jabs his index finger at my desk. "Have you accomplished anything today?"

SHALLOW: He frowns at me.

DEEP POV: His lips turned downward. "Oh."

SHALLOW: She wears a long frown.

DEEP POV: The corners of her mouth drooped.

SHALLOW: Elena frowned, looking thoughtful. (Cliché)

DEEP POV: With hunched shoulders, Elena slumped in the chair.

SHALLOW: Her expression frowned.

DEEP POV: She hesitated, blinking rapidly.

Alternatives for grimaced:

SHALLOW: I felt my face grimace.

DEEP POV: With my lips compressed, my heartbeat thundered in my ears.

SHALLOW: Anna grimaced when I touched her and demanded my money.

DEEP POV: Anna flinched when I gripped her arm. "Pardon me," I said, my sharp nails slicing into her soft flesh. "But you still owe me two hundred bucks."

SHALLOW: He had been shot and his face grimaced.

DEEP POV: He rubbed his collarbone, his breath coming in quick, whining gasps. "I—I've been shot."

Alternatives for wince / flinch:

SHALLOW: Heath winced when I startled him.

DEEP POV: Heath recoiled, his hand clutching his chest. "Sheesh, don't sneak up on me like that."

SHALLOW: Grant flinched.

DEEP POV: Grant gritted his teeth, cringing at the sight of all the blood.

SHALLOW: Clara's whole body flinched in revulsion.

DEEP POV: Clara recoiled, stumbling over her feet in an effort to get away.

Alternatives for pouted:

SHALLOW: Jackson wore a pouty expression. (Cliché)

DEEP POV: Jackson's shoulders slumped. "Fine. Kill the girl."

SHALLOW: Ruby looked disappointed and her bottom lip pouted.

DEEP POV: Ruby rubbed her hand over her face and turned away. "I didn't wanna go bear hunting anyway."

SHALLOW: Kent was pouting about the cookies.

DEEP POV: Kent's bottom lip thrust upward. "Can I have another cookie, please?"

SHALLOW: She moped, wanting to buy the ring.

DEEP POV: Her sexy lower lip extended just slightly past the top. "C'mon, luv, buy me that diamond ring."

Alternatives for sighing:

SHALLOW: Christian sighed with disapproval. (Cliché)

DEEP POV: Christian exhaled through tight lips.

SHALLOW: She let out a long, heavy sigh of defeat. (Cliché)

DEEP POV: Her whole body sagged. "Just drink my blood, Edward."

SHALLOW: Bella released a sigh of relief. (Cliché)

DEEP POV: Bella's tense posture relaxed. "Okay, you win."

SHALLOW: She was sighing and looking defeated.

DEEP POV: Her long, lowered eyelashes emanated a kind of surrender, and she let the breath swoosh from her lungs.

Alternatives for blushed / flushed:

SHALLOW: Buffy was blushing when she told us that she only killed vampires.

DEEP POV: Wringing her hands, Buffy leaned forward. "I swear I *only* kill vampires. They're not even really people."

SHALLOW: He blushed hotly and said Amanda was a liar.

DEEP POV: He twisted the pen between his index finger and his thumb, heat blazing in his cheeks. "Amanda's a liar."

SHALLOW: Drake's face looked flushed.

DEEP POV: Drake's forehead was damp with sweat and both his cheeks had red splotches like a circus clown.

SHALLOW: She looked nervous and her face was flushed red.

DEEP POV: She let out a nervous peal of laughter, then covered her mouth. "Sorry. I don't know what came over me."

SHALLOW: I was nervous and my I felt my face blush because I hated first dates.

DEEP POV: I fidgeted with zipper on my jacket. "Um, well, I'm not real good at first dates."

SHALLOW: I felt embarrassed and my face blushed.

DEEP POV: Blood flowed into my face, reddening my neck all the way up to my hairline.

SHALLOW: Julianna felt her face flush with color.

DEEP POV: Julianna's face colored fiercely, and her voice sounded edgy. "I, um, knew that."

SHALLOW: She felt her neck and ears blush.

DEEP POV: Her neck and ears turned scarlet like a sunburn.

Did this chapter give you some clever ideas on revising any bland descriptions?

The examples should inspire writers to create their own alternatives to overused facial expressions and gestures.

SHALLOW: ANTAGONISM

Quote: "Instead of stating a situation flat out, you want to let the reader discover what you're trying to say by watching a character in action and by listening to his/her dialogue. *Showing* brings your characters to life." —*bestselling author, Janet Evanovich*

This chapter will demonstrate how writers can *show* opposition or hostility toward another character through the expressions and body language of a villain or another opposing character. It is also a great way to reveal insight into your antagonist or even the mighty hero. These tips and tools should also help you revise any fight scenes. The examples will "show" how to convey the aggression through the Deep POV method to strengthen your writing.

Let's start with expressive body movements and animated gestures that are commonly used to signal aggression toward another character. Outward aggression can be shown in the facial expression, from judgmental frowns and puckered lips to snickers and full-on growls. The character's eyes can be used to convey a threat through a bold stare, and body temperature can increase as well to show heated cheeks and a sweaty brow.

When someone is about to attack another character, they usually give a visible signal such as clenching their fists, or spreading their feet apart for stability, or they might get red in the face. A character might pace with restlessness, or invade the personal space of the hero in a display of aggression by the villain.

Some physical signs of aggression might be:

Clenched teeth and jaws

Pointing or jabbing with a finger

Shaking body

Clenched fists

Rapid breathing/sharp drawing in breath

Rigid posture

Restlessness, fidgeting

Flushed face or extreme paleness of face

Verbal threats

Examples on how to revise shallow writing:

SHALLOW: I was so angry at Leo that I wanted to punch him.

DEEP POV: My body shook and my fingers curled into tight fists.

SHALLOW: Major looked furious and he lifted his chin in angry defiance. (cliché)

DEEP POV: The tip of Major's ears reddened, and he lifted his chin a notch to stare down at me like a bug he wanted to smash under the heel of his sneaker.

SHALLOW: I was very angry and I wanted to kick Charles in the face.

DEEP POV: I raised both hands, my fists clenched as if ready to strike, and took a boxer's stance.

SHALLOW: Carl looked extremely aggressive and moved his arms in an angry way.

DEEP POV: Carl's chest puffed out and he wildly waved his hands around as he spoke.

Please study and compare these longer examples…

SHALLOW: Miguel marched in outraged strides in front of me and then he moved closer to me.

DEEP POV: Miguel stomped back and forth like a jumpy tiger, until he unexpectedly spun on his booted heel and stepped right up to me.

Please study this longer example of aggression…

SHALLOW: I angrily went into the building, and flung open the door. Then I heatedly marched to his desk and used my arm to slide everything off the desk.

DEEP POV: I burst into the building, the door swinging open and banging into the wall. Huffing, I stomped over to my boss's desk and with one brutal sweep of my arm, slid everything off the surface and onto the floor.

★★★

Try not to clutter your prose with too many filter words that will convey obvious information like aggression. The fact that the character or villain was antagonistic should be understood by the reader without being bluntly told. Use all of these illustrations to spark your own creative muse!

SHALLOW: INDIFFERENCE

Quote: "Truly emotionless characters are tricky to pull off because outside of programming, brainwashing, and curses, you can't really have motivation or conflict without emotion. Even a truly evil villain, hellbent on destruction, is probably motivated by hate, fear, greed, or disgust. That said, indifference will be easier to work with, because the emotion can be there and just muted or very well hidden..." —*anonymous, Writing Questions Answered blog*

Indifference is an emotion or a forced reaction that a character might use to hide their true feelings. It can mean a lack of concern, boredom, disinterest, apathy, or nonchalance in any given situation. To add an extra layer of depth to the characterization, a writer could have one character who is compassionate and generous, and another who is indifferent and detached. This can add some great conflict and tension whenever these two diverse characters are on the same page together.

An indifferent character might actually be trying to disguise a deep hurt or emotional scar, so they pretend not to care and appear detached, flippant, and even sarcastic. This type of complex character might even be an outsider or recluse, who believes no one else will understand their pain or circumstances.

For instance, in a romance novel, a character that is cynical and indifferent (makes a good character growth ARC) might be protecting themselves by keeping the love interest at arm's length or closing off their heart to avoid getting hurt.

Some shallow words for indifference or boredom can be *glazed, tortured, listless, detached, remote, etc.* but these weak visualizes should be revised whenever possible with Deeper POV.

Signs of indifference might be:

Yawning loudly

Half-open eyelids

Rolling eyes

Shrugging shoulders

Sighing heavily

Limp posture / relaxed muscles

Head down or held in hands

Slouching in a seat or slumping in chair

Waving hand in the air dismissively

Glance up at the ceiling

Examples on how to revise shallow writing:

SHALLOW: I was bored listening to his stories at summer camp. They were so monotonous that I didn't listen.

DEEP POV: With my lips compressed, I slouched lower in my seat and ignored him.

SHALLOW: She felt detached from the lecture her mother gave and said, "I don't care."

DEEP POV: Her eyes rolled up. "Whatever."

SHALLOW: His expression looked bored.

DEEP POV: He yawned and closed his eyes.

SHALLOW: Tara was bored of answering questions.

DEEP POV: With a loud yawn, Tara said, "Well, I don't know."

SHALLOW: I didn't have time for a lecture on driving too fast.

DEEP POV: I crossed my legs and folded my arms. "Get to the point."

SHALLOW: Erin felt detached from the conversation and said in a dull voice, "I do not want to hear anymore."

DEEP POV: Erin sagged in his seat and sighed heavily. "I've heard enough."

SHALLOW: Lisa talked about her new boyfriend and I found it boring to listen to.

DEEP POV: I blinked, trying to keep my eyes open and not fall asleep while Lisa droned on about her new boyfriend.

SHALLOW: He thought the movie was dreary and mind-numbing. "I'm bored to tears," he said in an uninterested voice.

DEEP POV: His head fell back against the seat and he stared at the theater ceiling. "If I have to watch any more of this nonsense, I'm going to shoot myself."

SHALLOW: Billy looked at the wall while I was talking and I thought it was rude.

DEEP POV: Billy seemed to be spacing out, so I grabbed his arm and gave it a shake. "Don't tune me out again."

***

The following two examples demonstrate first what your sentences might look like with an annoying, visible narrator *telling* the story, and then what the writing might look like without the narrator.

Please closely examine these two scenes...

SHALLOW:

The long car ride to Aunt Jenny's house was uninteresting. There was nothing to do, but look out the window at the trees and houses and other cars. I was so bored that I thought about taking a nap. But then my dad tried to talk to me about school, but that was a dull subject.

I tried changing the radio station to hear some better music yet I couldn't find anything to fight the boredom, so got out my phone and texted my friend.

DEEP POV:

This had to be the longest car ride *ever*. Not much to do, but gaze out the window at the passing cars, and count the number of houses and trees whizzing by. When that become mind-numbing, I sighed and closed my eyes.

"How's that advanced math class you're taking this semester?" my dad asked.

"Fine," I said, opening my eyes. *There goes my nap.* "And the semester's over."

My dad glanced at me. "What about that art class—"

"Why don't we listen to some tunes," I suggested, changing the subject. I was seriously burned out on talking about school.

I switched radio stations until that proved futile. Only static or uninteresting talk shows, which equaled *yawn-fest.* I whipped out my cell phone and texted my best friend. She always had amusing stories that would help the time go by faster.

***

As you start to revise your own stories, remember that it is easy to inadvertently violate the *show, don't tell* principle when you're writing early drafts.

SHALLOW: COLDNESS

Quote: "Personality plays a large role in how a characters sounds. Their voice will reflect that personality and color every line of dialog and internal thought." —*author and blogger, Janice Hardy*

If a writer tells the reader that a character is cold or it was a cold day, it is considered shallower writing. Writers should find innovative ways to *show* through Deeper POV instead.

Everything a writer needs to set the scene and vividly describe a location or feeling for the reader can be accomplished by using sensory details. As a writer revises a scene, it is effective to imagine themselves in the actual location, then think about the details. *What is the character seeing, smelling, hearing, and touching?* Using the five senses is mandatory when a writer wants to put a clear, descriptive visual into the reader's mind.

Coldness in a character usually indicates a decrease in body temperature, or fear, or even an illness. And it can be used to describe the weather or how an object feels to the touch, but writers should illustrate it in a vibrant way that a reader will easily be able to imagine.

To revise any shallower writing, I would look for phrases such as, *he felt cold* or *I could feel the cold* or *it was a cold day.*

Some physical signs of coldness might be:

Trembling legs

Hugging one's body

Quivering lips

Blue skin

Teeth chattering

Chills shake body

Runny nose

Numb fingers or toes

Shivering body

Stuttering dialogue

Examples of cold weather for settings:

Frost on the windows

Howling winds

Birds flying south

Heavy fog

Overcast skies

Spiders spinning larger than usual webs

Ice on the ground

Icicles hanging from roof

Slick roads

Harsh rains

Bare trees

Somber clouds

Examples on how to revise shallow writing:

SHALLOW: When I went outside, I felt very cold today. I put on a jacket against the wind.

DEEP POV: The second I stepped out of the house, an icy wind slapped my bare skin. Shivering, I yanked on my wool coat and stuffed my hands into warm gloves.

SHALLOW: Liam was freezing while he worked outside. His hands felt cold as he shoveled the snow out of driveway. He wished he had put on mittens.

DEEP POV: Liam's fingers felt numb and his nose ran. He shoveled another heap of snow from the driveway and cursed at himself for forgetting to wear mittens.

SHALLOW: It was cold in the classroom and the heater was broken.

DEEP POV: Thick frost clung to the windows of the classroom, and my legs trembled. If the teacher didn't get that heater fixed soon, I was coming to school in skiing gear!

SHALLOW: Even though Emma wore a jacket, the weather felt really cold.

DEEP POV: Huddling inside her warm jacket, Emma's breath made little white puffs in the frosty air.

SHALLOW: The weather in October is extremely cold and it makes me shiver.

DEEP POV: My teeth are chattering, and I shove my hands deep into my pockets against the chilly October weather.

SHALLOW: Mason opened the door of the spaceship and some very frosty air came out. He felt cold and shivered.

DEEP POV: An arctic gust escaped the pod when Mason opened the door of the spaceship. He shivered and pulled up the collar of his coat, and then rubbed his hands together to get warmer.

SHALLOW: It was a cold, overcast day at the campsite.

DEEP POV: The wintry morning sent a glacial coldness around the camp.

Here are a few longer scenes on how to use Deep POV to describe the cold. (In the shallow example, I did not underline the shallower writing, but see if you can clearly identify it now that you're more aware of *showing* vs. *telling*.)

Please study and compare these examples…

SHALLOW: It had heavily snowed last night, and I need to walk with slow steps on the sidewalk so I don't fall down. I feel really cold. I notice the cars, houses, and street have lots of new snow on them.

DEEP POV: Outside everything is white. The world resembles a frozen wasteland with a fresh blanket of snow covering the street from last night's blizzard. I move slowly along the icy sidewalks, wrapping my arms around my torso to stay warm. Even the snow-bound cars seem abandoned today.

Please study and compare these examples...

SHALLOW: I built a snowman and then put a hat on its head. It started snowing and the cold made my lips feel numb.

DEEP POV: When I'd finished building my awesome snowman, I put a black hat on his white round head and smiled. A fresh swirl of powdery snowflakes danced in the intermittent gusts, and I caught sight of my quivering, blue lips in the window.

Please study and compare these examples...

SHALLOW: The air-conditioner was set to high and Olivia did not know how to turn it off. She felt cold and shaky. Her hands were the coldest part of her body.

DEEP POV: Olivia licked her dry, cracked lips and blew into her cupped hands for warmth. The air-conditioner was blasting in her office and she wasn't sure how to turn the dang thing off!

***

Here is a longer, more detailed scene showing that a character feels cold and it also describes the setting. Please closely examine this scene to get a clear indication on how to describe the cold weather and the feeling of being cold.

DEEP POV:

The burning sensation spreading on the bare skin of his arms and legs, along with his face and neck had started to get worse. Despite its angelic appearance, the icy sleet felt as though Ethan was being stabbed with thousands of sharp needles.

"I *never* should've told Amy that I wanted to see other people on her birthday," he mumbled.

It was shortly after that ill-timed statement that his girlfriend had jumped into the car and sped off. She'd left him outside of town without a jacket (he'd given it to her to wear), gloves, or a cell phone, when they'd stopped to make a snowman.

Yeah, she was 100% pissed off, and now because of his big mouth, he was going to freeze to death.

He sighed. He *had* to make it home before nightfall.

Ethan stomped in sodden boots through the knee-deep drifts, hugging himself against the subzero winds. The snow was falling incessantly and blurred the hills and rooftops in the valley below. He flexed his hands and swiped at his runny nose with stiff fingers.

The fluffy snowflakes drifting downward would make a pretty Christmas card, but the cold seemed to penetrate his flesh and pierce the very marrow of his bones.

Ethan shivered uncontrollably and his body was shaken with a wheezing cough. He searched the surrounding area with teary eyes for some trace of shelter to stay the night. But there wasn't a building in sight.

Just great. I'll look like a snowman myself by morning.

With each lumbering step, his toes tingled with pain, and the soft crunch of snow beneath his boots echoed in the dying light. The roads were icy and his feet slipped on the slick surface. Ethan stumbled down the hill toward the city lights blinking like a rescue beacon in the distance.

After drudging for miles, he fell to his knees in exhaustion. The snow steadily enveloped him in a powdery white blanket that would surely cover his frozen corpse.

***

These examples should spark your creative muse. And if you use the Deep POV technique to describe the cold, then I can guarantee your readers will notice an amazing difference in your stories.

SHALLOW: FATIGUED

Quote: "Description, *your* description, paints in the story-world just as a reader is walking through it. For the reader, the story-world doesn't exist before the moment he/she encounters it..." — *fiction editor, Beth Hill of "A Novel Edit"* (I had the honor to work with Beth on my adult PNR novel, IMMORTAL ECLIPSE, and she's an amazing editor.)

When your character is tired or fatigued, I would *show* the character's mental and physical exhaustion through Deeper POV. I realize that it is much simpler to just state that a character is drowsy or that a character looks exhausted, but I think it is much more fun to *show* the reader instead—*don't you?*

Exhaustion can come from many different things, such as an illness or depression. It can cause a character to use poor judgment or be a side effect of prescription drugs, and in some cases, dehydration may even be to blame. Stress and insomnia can also be major factors of extreme fatigue.

In this chapter, I have put together some examples to further explain what I mean. Please use them as a reference and inspiration for your own stories.

Some physical signs of exhaustion might be:

Loud yawning

Heavy eyelids

Droopy eyelids

Weakness in limbs

Cannot concentrate

Bloodshot eyes

Dark circles under the eyes

A disheveled appearance

Clumsiness

Slurred speech

Examples on how to revise shallow writing:

SHALLOW: I feel so exhausted from running the marathon.

DEEP POV: My legs wobble and a bout of dizziness strikes my senses when I finish running the marathon.

SHALLOW: When Clary saw Noah still wearing last night's clothes, she realized that he hadn't slept at all.

DEEP POV: Noah lumbered into the house like a zombie. His shirt and pants were wrinkled, and his face unshaven. He must've been up all night studying.

SHALLOW: I yawned, and then I went into the bathroom to put cold water on my face because I was so sleepy. My eyes looked tired in the mirror.

DEEP POV: Yawning loudly, I stumbled into the bathroom and splashed cold water on my face. My reflection in the mirror revealed bags under my bloodshot eyes.

SHALLOW: I felt sleepy and worn-out.

DEEP POV: My movements were heavy and sluggish like I was trudging through snow.

SHALLOW: Sophia felt so drowsy that she tried to not fall asleep during the lecture.

DEEP POV: Sophia rubbed at her eyes with tiny fists and fought to stay awake during the longwinded lecture.

SHALLOW: I wanted to go back to bed because I was so weary from being up with the baby.

DEEP POV: My body swayed and I dragged my feet into the dark bedroom. As I fell over into the softness of the comforter and pillow, my drooping eyelids instantly closed.

SHALLOW: Dan looked sleepy and he fell asleep in class. He started snoring loudly. The teacher got mad and woke him up.

DEEP POV: Dan's breathing slowed and his eyelids grew heavy. He rested his head on the desk and his eyes closed. He must've been snoring, because the teacher shook him awake.

SHALLOW (*cannot yawn dialogue*): "No, I'm awake," I yawned.

DEEP POV: "No, I'm awake," I muttered, yawning and stretching my weary limbs.

SHALLOW: She felt lethargic, but worry prevented her from falling asleep.

DEEP POV: She sagged onto a chair with a glazed look in her eyes. Sleep would be impossible now.

SHALLOW: I was exhausted and sat on the sofa. I could probably sleep standing up. (Cliché.) I closed my eyes and went to sleep.

DEEP POV: Collapsing onto the sofa, my eyes drifted shut. My whole body sagged into the cushions and sleep came quickly.

***

Here are two longer examples of showing an exhausted character. (In the shallow example, I did not underline the shallower writing, but see if you can clearly identify it now that you're more aware of *showing* vs. *telling*.)

Please closely examine these two scenes...

SHALLOW (info-dump):

Aaron felt very tired. He wanted to go to sleep, but he had to wait up until his little brother got home from the birthday party. He tried to stay awake by turning up the sound on the TV, but it did not help him stay awake.

Aaron went into the kitchen and he made some coffee. He hoped that the caffeine would keep him from falling asleep. His mom counted on him to look after his younger brother while she worked nights, but he was too young at seventeen to be like a parent to his brother. When the coffee was ready, he drank a lot of cups, and then he felt more awake.

He heard the front door open as Aaron entered the living room. Now his brother was finally home, and he could to sleep.

DEEP POV:

Aaron yawned and sank lower on the couch. His lids, heavy with fatigue, gradually began to close and his body seemed to liquefy into the softness of the sofa. He had the urge to go upstairs and climb into bed, but he had to wait until his little brother, Gabe, got home from the birthday party.

"Wake up," he said aloud to the empty room. "Do *not* fall asleep, Aaron."

His mom would kill him if he did.

He sat up and grabbed the TV remote. Aaron cranked the volume on the western he'd been watching, but within seconds, his head fell back onto the headrest.

No, no, no. Stay awake!

The seventeen-year-old stood and stretched, then shuffled into the kitchen. He made a pot of strong coffee and leaned against the counter, the floor cold beneath his bare feet.

Aaron glanced at the clock on the wall. Only eleven. His mom wouldn't be home for hours from the hospital. Since she'd started working the graveyard shift, she counted on him to look after Gabe.

"This sucks," he grumbled. "I'm too young to act like Gabe's damn parent. It isn't fair."

When the coffee finished brewing, he poured himself a steaming mug. Aaron gulped down three cups until the caffeine buzz jolted his system.

The front door clicked open as Aaron walked into the living room. Finally, Gabe was home and Aaron could hit the sack.

***

The tools in this chapter should help writers rework any shallower writing that appears in early drafts. And I would study the work of other authors in your genre to get ideas on phrasing and sentence structure, and also inspiration for characterization.

SHALLOW: PAIN

Quote: "Creating character emotions remains one of my toughest challenges as a budding novelist. To truly show these characters and put them forth on the screen [or in a book] as though they were living and breathing, without making it seem cardboard is in one word: a challenge." —*writer and blogger, Casey Herringshaw*

For many writers, trying to describe pain or discomfort can be difficult. Even though pain is not an emotion, but more of a *feeling*, it should be described through a Deeper POV.

When trying to describe a character's pain to readers, writers should try to "show" the feeling by being descriptive enough to let the reader visualize what the character is experiencing while also respecting their intelligence, which means *showing* and not *telling*.

In order to make the reader empathetic to the character's pain, a writer should use metaphors or some specific language. To really convey the character's suffering (severe, throbbing, tender or sore, abrupt or intensifying), a writer can describe pain through the actions and reactions of the character.

For instance, if you're writing an intense fight scene, describing the pain of a kick or a punch to the face, should be short and to the point to keep the action moving forward. Or to deepen character-ization, a tough and apathetic type character might get shot, but only display pain by gritting their teeth. Alternatively, a wimpy or fearful character with any type of injury might whimper and cry over just stubbing their toe.

Some of the best advice I can give writers is to keep the reader "hooked" by *showing* the character's actions as opposed to stating them. If a character is injured, a writer can *show* the character gri-macing when he moves and rubbing his back, so the reader can just conclude that the character has back pain.

Some physical signs of pain might be:

Elevated blood pressure

Dilated pupil size

Perspire heavily

Hands and/or feet can be cold

Clenching or grinding the teeth

Covering, rubbing, or grabbing the pained area

Wincing when touched

Eyes that water or excess crying

Writhing or constant shifting in position

Moaning or groaning

Below, I've put together some examples of shallow writing com-pared to Deeper POV to show a character in pain rather than state it for the reader. None of my examples are terribly original, but they should give writers ideas on how to revise their own stories.

Now to be clear, I think it's perfectly fine to use the word "pain" in your writing if needed; however, anytime you can revise with Deeper POV, you should.

Examples on how to revise shallow writing:

SHALLOW: I felt tense with pain in my upper body.

DEEP POV: The tightness across my shoulders increased.

SHALLOW: He closed his eyes against the pain.

DEEP POV: A flicker of agony passed behind his closed lids.

SHALLOW: My head hurt with a bad headache.

DEEP POV: My brain felt like the hot mash of decaying potatoes.

SHALLOW: He thought the pain was bad.

DEEP POV: His pulse beat a tattoo at the base of his throat.

SHALLOW: I moved slowly to get to safety, but my body felt sore.

DEEP POV: I crawled to safety, a sensation of coldness lapped around my heart.

SHALLOW: He couldn't see very well when the pain increased.

DEEP POV: His vision went white with discomfort.

SHALLOW: The gunshot hurt and caused a lot of pain. She felt dizzy as the paramedic leaned over her body.

DEEP POV: The throbbing from the gunshot wound pulsed. Everything funneled, so she only glimpsed the paramedic's face above her.

SHALLOW: I wanted to cry from the pain of the hot poker as it hit my shoulder.

DEEP POV: My insides writhed when the hot poker struck my shoulder.

SHALLOW: The older man's expression looked distressed.

DEEP POV: The old man's face grimaced and he moaned.

SHALLOW: Jane felt a pain in her head.

DEEP POV: Jane rested her head in her hands and began to rub her temples.

SHALLOW: He laughed and felt a pain in his stomach.

DEEP POV: When he laughed, the ache in his belly flashed hard and quick.

SHALLOW: She had a bad pain in her side.

DEEP POV: If only her hips would stop aching.

Please study and compare these next two examples...

SHALLOW: I realized that I had a hard time concentrating on the test because I knew that I had a pain in my forehead. I thought if I took some pain medication it would help my headache.

DEEP POV: I clenched my teeth and rubbed my temple. The sharp throbbing spread across my forehead, blooming into a full-blown headache. I needed aspirin and *quick* if I hoped to pass the test.

***

I have included two longer scenes that provide an illustration on how to *show* pain. (In the shallow example, I did not underline the obvious areas of shallower writing, but see if you can easily spot it.)

Please carefully compare these examples...

SHALLOW:

I felt the knife stab into my skin and then the man plunged it deeper into my stomach. The pain was intense and the knife felt like it was sinking into my organs, and then there was a horrible, excruciating feeling of pain. I felt my eyes roll into the back of my head as the knife was suddenly pulled out of my flesh. Then I panicked as I put my hands over my wound, because I felt desperate to slow the blood that was rushing out. The blood went straight through my fingers and I saw it hit the ground.

Bland paragraphs like the one above reveal a practice that's very common with new writers, where they not only tend to overwrite, but state facts in a bland way. Please closely examine this scene rewritten...

DEEP POV:

The knife speared my stomach, and I stumbled backward as the searing force seemed to strike every nerve in my body. A taste of bile rose in my throat. The man advanced and thrust the blade in deeper, striking my organs. I hissed out a breath and fell to my knees. My vision blurred when the knife was jerked from my flesh.

Instinctively, I placed my hands over the wound, but the flow of blood seeped through my fingers and hit the ground like a thick, scarlet stream of death.

***

This chapter should give writers some clever ideas on how to rewrite any shallower scenes. And please take all of these suggestions to heart, and *only* make the changes that you feel will best suit your writing style and story.

SHALLOW: WARMTH

Quote: "You might be an amateur if you rely too heavily on clichés. This item is obligatory for any writing handbook. Beware the automatic phrase, such as "white as snow" and "quiet as a mouse." If your heroic character roars like a lion, she'd better be a lioness."— *author, James V. Smith, Jr.*

It is bland and cliché to state that it was a hot day or that the character felt warm. Body temperature can fluctuate depending on the circumstances and the setting, so writers should use Deep POV to describe the sensation or the warmer climate.

Whether a writer is describing the weather, or how something feels to the touch, or if a character feels warm, the more detailed the descriptions are, the better your storytelling skills will become. A number of different things can cause a person to become warm such as, anxiety, nervousness, weather, embarrassment, and illness.

Certain types of genres require varied levels of detail when establishing the setting and world-building. For example, a high-fantasy, historical adventure, or a science fiction novel will have an observant readership that expects not only graphic details and powerful imaginary regarding the setting, but facts and accuracy, too. One way to convey the weather or depict the setting is to have a character describe the background in his/her own "voice" through the five senses, rather than using an omniscient POV.

And I urge writers not to describe the setting with a cliché such as, "It was a dark and stormy night..." because settings can establish a distinct mood and atmosphere, like in a gothic novel with a mysterious castle, or a spaceship in a galaxy far, far away. Consider the setting not just as a factual location, but as a crucial part of a story's ambiance and emotional impact.

Some physical signs of warmth might be:

Heavy sweating

A flushed or red appearance to the skin

Panting, gasping, or wheeziness

Slick-sweat hair

Feeling lethargic or drowsy

Heavy-eyed

Dizziness

Nausea / Vomiting

Thirsty

Examples of warm weather for settings:

Wilting flowers

Brown, dead grass

Cloudless sky

Bright, hot sun

Humid

Dry winds

Sizzling asphalt

Air-conditioned house

Condensation on glasses

Sunburned faces / bodies

Muggy heat

Examples on how to revise shallow writing:

SHALLOW: When I left the house and the sun felt hot.

DEEP POV: Outside, the sun warmed my skin.

SHALLOW: He felt hot under the desert sun.

DEEP POV: The blazing desert sun beat down on him like the fires of hell.

SHALLOW: My skin was too hot and it looked red like a sunburn.

DEEP POV: My skin turned a splotchy red and felt fiery to the touch.

SHALLOW: She felt too warm, so she decided to go swimming in the pool.

DEEP POV: Her feverish skin cooled when she jumped into the swimming pool.

SHALLOW: The day was hot and sunny.

DEEP POV: The bright sunshine flared in the sky like a fiery ball.

SHALLOW: The summer weather was humid and hot.

DEEP POV: It was another torrid day. The brown lawns appeared shriveled and dry and the flowers wilted like sleepy children.

SHALLOW: The day was too hot and the sky looked very blue.

DEEP POV: The sun hotly glares down from a cloudless cobalt sky.

SHALLOW: I felt sweaty and thirsty.

DEEP POV: Sweat poured down my face and a deep thirst plagued my senses.

SHALLOW: She walked slowly in the heat to a fan.

DEEP POV: She moved sluggishly through the stifling air to the fan.

SHALLOW: The street looked really warm.

DEEP POV: Steam rose in blurry waves from the black-tarred streets.

SHALLOW: I looked up at the hot sun that was shining on the homes.

DEEP POV: I squinted at the blazing sun that violently shown down upon the houses.

SHALLOW: The dog looked hot and he was panting.

DEEP POV: The dog panted, its tongue hung down in an effort to stay cool.

SHALLOW: The sunny day felt scorching.

DEEP POV: The sun flared like a furnace with no gentle winds to relieve its fiery wrath.

SHALLOW: I heard the sound of insects buzzing in the heat.

DEEP POV: The buzz of the cicadas emanated their somber drone of summer's blistering oppression.

Here are two more examples of shallow writing and revising with a Deeper POV. (In the shallow example, I did not underline the shallower writing, but see if you can clearly identify it now that you're more aware of *showing* vs. *telling*.)

Please closely examine these two short scenes…

SHALLOW:

It was a very hot day in August. Everyone felt warm and looked miserable. I noticed that no one moved or wanted to go outside. It was too hot to do much of anything. Even the animals did not like the heat.

I stood at the front window and looked outside as I placed my face against the window. The glass felt cold to touch because my mom had the air-conditioner turned on. The street appeared hot outside, too.

DEEP POV:

Everything appeared to melt from the heat of the sweltering August sun, and even the sizzling asphalt resembled black liquid in the blaze of the afternoon glare. Heat waves were modulating off the pavement, just like I imagined the streets of Hell.

Nothing stirred. Not even the birds, squirrels, or dogs.

Sweat glistened on my skin and I pressed my warm face against the cool, perspiring glass of the living room window. Thank goodness, my mom had cranked up the air-conditioning.

***

Whenever possible, be specific in your descriptions. Use vivid metaphors and similes to create dazzling images. For example, offer vibrant, colorful details by describing the heat of the sun, and then how it affects the character's senses in a scene that features warmer weather.

SHALLOW: THOUGHTFUL

Quote: "Complexity is an indispensable ingredient of life, and so it ought to be with the characters we create in our stories. Paradoxes do not negate the consistencies, they simply add to them. Characters are more interesting if they are made up of mixed stuff, if they have warring elements." —*author, Stavros Halvatzis*

Just stating that a character looked thoughtful or was contemplative seems unoriginal and boring in my humble opinion. Books need some conflict or tension within the storyline, or a reader might put down the book and never pick it up again. If a writer states an expression or feeling or mode of thought, then it is *telling*—and too much telling is tedious to read.

A thoughtful character might be considered an intelligent person, who weighs the pros and cons before making any rash decisions. Or a tense character who likes to overanalyze events within the narrative could be depicted as brooding or pensive.

When someone looks thoughtful, the face is usually relatively neutral, although there can be a hint of a frown that tends to suggest concentration. The eyes are fixed on a wall, or staring off, and the lips are taut. If the person has a trace of a smile or he/she occasionally nods their head, this would indicate listening with interest.

One way to stay in close-and-personal (and there are many!) is to try to reduce as many filtering references as you can from your writing. Examples of shallow words are: *brooding, pensive, contemplative, reflective, introspective, wistful, deep in thought, comprehending, quizzical, curious, inquiring, puzzled, perplexed, confused,* etc.

Signs of thoughtfulness might be:

Unblinking eyes

Chewing lower lip

Staring into space

Quiet, not talking

Running hand through hair

Drumming fingers

Rubbing back of the neck

Tapping a foot

Furrowing brow

Eyebrows slanted or slightly raised

Examples on how to revise shallow writing:

SHALLOW: I was thoughtful as I contemplated with curiosity, then I asked what happened next.

DEEP POV: With my elbow on the table, I made a fist and rested my cheek on it. "Then what happened?"

SHALLOW: Lauren considered the situation thoughtfully. "So really?"

DEEP POV: Lauren tugged on her earlobes. "That really happened?"

SHALLOW: I was pensive while I reflected on my options.

DEEP POV: I stared down at my hands while trying to decide what to do next.

SHALLOW: She comprehended the problem, and then she said thoughtfully, "That is interesting."

DEEP POV: She posed a finger under her chin. "Hmmm, interesting."

SHALLOW: I felt confused and I was struggling over the dilemma.

DEEP POV: I laced my fingers under my chin and frowned. *There had to be a solution!*

SHALLOW: Giles felt puzzled and confused. "I do not understand."

DEEP POV: Giles pinched the bridge of his nose. "I am quite flummoxed."

SHALLOW: I felt perplexed. "Are you sure it was a UFO?" I asked quizzically.

DEEP POV: I paced the room with my hands behind my back. "You *sure* it was a real UFO?"

SHALLOW: Thomas looked wistful. (cliché)

DEEP POV: Thomas fingered his jowl, and then said, "I've got it!"

SHALLOW: I was introspective about the movie.

DEEP POV: I scratched my head still unsure that I enjoyed the film.

SHALLOW: He looked deep in thought. (Cliché)

DEEP POV: He rubbed his baldhead. "You're not making this easy!"

Next, I have provided two longer scenes of Deep POV vs. shallower writing. (I have underlined what I consider to be to be shallower writing in the first example.)

Please carefully examine these two examples…

SHALLOW:

There was three girls sitting in the high school cafeteria, and they were discussing the upcoming funeral and the party planned for afterwards.

The cafeteria looked really big and the girls heard lots of loud sounds. There were gross smells, too. The girls looked thoughtful while they considered what to do about the party. The three girls had heard that Nicki Button had been stabbed that morning and she would no longer be attending school, because she was no longer alive.

"We just need to pick out the invitations, thank you gifts, and alcohol for the party," Bonnie said thoughtfully. "But I don't know —do you two girls think an iPod, a black T-shirt, and Gloria Vanderbilt perfume is too boring?" she asked nervously.

"I think it is perfect," Charlotte said excitedly. "I mean, think how cool it is to have the newest technology, plus black clothing to wear, and a new fragrance?"

Bonnie nodded contemplatively. "Completely," she agreed seriously. "Plus, black doesn't show stains."

Which was good when there was a stain of blood on your clothes from killing someone, Bonnie thought.

"Hey, what about my idea?" Kathy inquired, looking upset. "I said we needed to have some chocolate, too!"

"That's too expensive to add now," Charlotte argued soberly.

"And too much work to do that." Bonnie sighed broodingly.

She did not really care about the party stuff. She knew she had a knife with blood on it to hide before her next class, she thought.

Kathy and Charlotte watched Bonnie lift her purse, open it up, and then take out a lipstick from her bag. She began to put it onto her lips.

"Where did you get that lipstick? Is that Nicki's?" Kathy asked with surprise.

Bonnie appeared indifferent. "I took it because she cannot use it now that she is dead," she said thoughtfully.

Did you see how bland and flat the writing was in the first scene?

It is boring for readers to be "told" what each character is thinking or feeling; and all those dialogue tags with emotional qualifiers are like red flags that the writing needs further revision.

Please study this revised version with "voice" and sensory details.

DEEP POV:

Three girls sat in the high school cafeteria, discussing the upcoming funeral after-party. The chatter around them seemed almost deafening. A fellow classmate Emily Emerson had been stabbed that morning, and the school was buzzing with murderous gossip. The stench of greasy food hung heavily in the air, making Bonnie wrinkle her nose.

She hated hamburger Thursdays.

"I can't believe Emily's dead!" Kathy was sniffling and dapping at her teary eyes with a napkin.

"Believe it," Bonnie said with a yawn. "Now onto more important topics. We need to finish picking out the invitations, gift bags, and champagne for the after-party." She tapped her chin with a sparkly blue finger. "I just don't know—do you guys think an iPod, a black T-shirt, and Gloria Vanderbilt perfume is too non-mourning?"

"I think it's perfect." Charlotte sat up straighter and smiled. "I mean, think how cool it is to have the newest technology, plus dark clothing for the funeral, and a new fragrance. It totally makes the whole dreary funeral less morbid."

Bonnie nodded. "I completely agree. Plus, black doesn't show stains."

Which was always a plus when there was blood on your clothes from your latest killing spree.

"Hey, what about my idea?" Kathy pouted, her bottom lip protruding "*I* said we needed have chocolate, too. It's comfort food…"

Charlotte shook her head. "That's way too expensive to add now."

"And too much work," Bonnie agreed.

As if she cared about the gift bags when she had a bloody knife to stash before her next class.

Charlotte gasped when Bonnie extracted a tube of Chanel lipstick from her Kate Spade bag and smeared the glossy texture over her lips.

Kathy's eyebrows shot up to her hairline. "Isn't that Emily's?"

Bonnie shrugged and tossed the lipstick back into her purse. "I stole it from her locker before lunch." When the two girls stared at her in silence, she rolled her blue eyes. "What's the big deal? It's not like she's going to need it anymore—*she's dead.*"

***

After reading the two examples, writers should be able to grasp how *naming the emotion*, too many "emotional qualifiers," and adverbs can make the prose stale and boring for readers.

SHALLOW: STUBBORN

Quote: "The "difficult" female character can—and will—do the shocking, the unexpected and, as a consequence, will give your story an immediate jolt of energy. She is the character who doesn't fit the mold." —*bestselling author, Ruth Harris*

With any type of characterization, I think it is better to "show" a character's personality and flaws throughout the storyline rather than be told that a character is rude, or sad, or even stubborn.

For example, in a lot of popular romance novels, the alpha male character and their leading lady will display the stubborn trait. Sometimes stubbornness is just a resistance to change in his/her life, which can work as a great "fatal flaw" if your character has to overcome a significant growth ARC.

Most stubborn people have trouble admitting when they are wrong, which can add a lot of tension within your storyline between characters. These types of personalities would rather argue and fight than suffer a blow to their ego.

However, just stating a character trait like, "Tom was a stubborn person," or whether the trait is a negative or positive one can cause narrative distance. And for me personally, I like getting to know the characters as the story progresses, and if it is directly stated, then it takes some of the enjoyment out of getting to know the characters.

Signs of stubbornness might be:

Thinned lips

A fixed stare

Clenched fists

Refusing to listen or agree

Both arms crossed

Place hands on hips

Deep frowns

Giving a sideways glance

A constant fear and sense of insecurity

Being afraid of change

Examples on how to revise shallow writing:

SHALLOW: He looked very angry and stubborn. "Damn it. There are no such things as ghosts!" he shouted loudly.

DEEP POV: He smacked his palm on the table with a force that rattled the dishes. When he spoke, Laura had to sit back, or she might've developed hearing loss. "*Damn it. There are no such things as ghosts!*"

SHALLOW: I was stalwart type of person and I did not like Demi bossing me around.

DEEP POV: I lifted my chin and looked her in the eye. "Stop bossing me around, Demi."

SHALLOW: Scott was a very tenacious person.

DEEP POV: Scott stood rigid with his wide shoulders back. "End of discussion."

SHALLOW: I refused to be bullied into going out tonight.

DEEP POV: I tossed hair over my shoulder. "Not gonna happen."

SHALLOW: Carol stubbornly declined to help Daryl bury the zombies.

DEEP POV: With both arms crossed, Carol shook her head. "It's *your* turn to bury the walkers, Daryl."

SHALLOW: Julie didn't understand why her sister was so obstinate.

DEEP POV: Julie stiffened at the challenge in her sister's eyes.

SHALLOW: I saw Alyson shake her head persistently.

DEEP POV: Alyson shook her head and backed away.

SHALLOW: He was determined to win the argument.

DEEP POV: His arms overlapped, resting against his broad muscular chest.

Here is an excerpt taken from my novel, SMASH INTO YOU, where the main character is faced with a hard choice, yet stubbornly refuses to submit to cruel hazing tactics that are being forced upon her by the sorority that she's trying to join.

Please carefully examine this scene…

DEEPER POV:

"There's no way I'm doing this," I said, backing away. "If I get caught, I'll get expelled."

"You already have so many infractions that your legacy status is the only thing keeping us from dropping you like a bad habit," Jade replied. "You're still on probation."

"You do realize what you're giving up if you don't do what we ask, right?" Brooklyn crossed her slim arms over her chest. "You'll *never* be one of us."

"You'll be alone," Claire said. "No sisters. No real social life. You might as well crawl back under the rock you clawed your way out of."

I stared hard at glassy-eyed Claire. "Did you grow your hair out just to cover up the three sixes on your scalp?"

Claire glared at me, but did not respond.

I wanted to be a Zeta Beta sister. I wanted Paris. But a girl had to draw the line somewhere. And this was the place. I was sick of them screwing with me.

"I'm not going to get a man fired," I said, finding the courage to look each one of them in the eye. "There are certain things I won't do to join a sorority."

"It's your funeral," Jade said. "We're having a chapter meeting next week to discuss some *issues* that have recently transpired with two pledges, and I expect you to attend."

Claire stepped forward. "And maybe you should consider de-pledging in front of the other girls that night. Everyone will want to know why we're renouncing your bid."

My legs quaked as I turned away from them. Turned away from the life I was so desperate to have. Turned my back on my Paris dreams. All because I stubbornly refused to participate in these humiliating traditions that the pledges were forced to do.

***

It is easy to "show" a stubborn character through their actions, reactions, and internal-monologue like shown in the excerpt above. Stubbornness is an interesting character flaw that can add a lot of tension to any storyline.

SHALLOW: DOUBT

Quote: "These emotions—fear, pain, doubt—are part of the human condition. If your hero is impervious to them, it is harder to understand them and harder to imagine ourselves as them." — *author, Tristan Gregory*

If you write mysteries, thrillers, or suspense, then this chapter should help you strengthen your storyline with a Deeper POV. Having a suspicious character(s) is a useful trope in almost any drama, even if that shady character turns out to be innocent.

Suspicion or doubt can take on many forms, like the unreliable narrator, and these traits can be another way to add a deeper layer of characterization to any fiction novel.

In order to realistically explain any suspicious characters, I would use a traumatic event from the characters' past, or something that happens plot wise to arouse your character's suspicion. (But be careful of it *not* becoming a sense of paranoia.)

Suspicion and doubt can also make a great "fatal flaw" for your character to overcome by the end of the story.

Doubt is closely tied with suspicion, but it can also be used to create unanswered questions about secondary characters or mysterious events throughout the storyline. It can also be used subtly throughout a narrative to build-up suspense.

Signs of doubt or suspicion might be:

Narrowed eyes

Brows drawing together

One eyebrow lifted

Squinty eyes

Long, hard stare

Throat clearing

Puckered lips

Nodding head

Folding arms

Stiff posture

Examples on how to revise shallow writing:

SHALLOW: I was doubtful that Shawn was telling me the truth.

DEEP POV: With narrowed eyes, I stared at Shawn. "Is that true?" I demanded.

SHALLOW: He felt doubtful about going on the vacation.

DEEP POV: He checked his bank statement, but the small number meant he probably couldn't go on the vacation.

SHALLOW: I did not believe Alex because he was a two-faced liar.

DEEP POV: My brows drew together and I sighed. "How can I trust anything you say?"

SHALLOW: I did not trust him and he was acting suspicious.

DEEP POV: I squinted at him and tilted my head to the side. "You're *not* fooling me."

SHALLOW: Maggie listened to Glenn's story with a shadow of doubt. (cliché)

DEEP POV: Maggie nodded her head while Glenn talked, but her gut instinct told her to be wary.

SHALLOW: I saw a strange, suspicious man outside.

DEEP POV: My posture stiffened when I glimpsed a strange man lurking outside.

SHALLOW: As a cop, Malcom didn't believe one word the suspect said.

DEEP POV: Malcom rolled his eyes heavenward and fingered the silver badge fastened to his belt.

***

Here is a condensed scene taken from my paranormal romance novel, UNDER SUNLESS SKIES, which depicts the feelings of doubt and suspicion in the main character. She is being blackmailed and everyone she knows seems like a suspect.

Please carefully examine this scene…

DEEP POV:

When I stop at my locker before third period, Tanisha Jackson, one of my good friends and fellow lovers of dark-side apparel, rushes up to me in the corridor.

"Hey! I'm glad I caught you," she says breathlessly.

"What's up?" I ask, opening the locker.

Lowering my sunglasses, I check my teeth for lipstick stains in the mirror, rubbing one finger over a red smudge on my front tooth. As I lean back, a black envelope flutters out of the locker, and I barely manage to catch it before it hits the ground.

"Can I borrow your notes for trig tomorrow?" Tanisha briefly touches my shoulder, and I glance at her. "I'm leaving early for a dentist appointment."

"Um, yeah, I guess…" I say distractedly.

"I don't even want to go because the last time I had an appointment," she says, "it was *so* annoying when the dental assistant asked me to remove my tongue ring…"

While Tanisha is talking, I rip open the envelope and pull out a white slip of paper with the typed words:

I KNOW YOUR SECRETS. TELL ANYONE ABOUT THIS NOTE, AND THEY BECOME PUBLIC KNOWLEDGE!

My hands shake as I scan the note, and then I reread it because I can't quite believe what I'm seeing. My chest tightens painfully. I just learned the truth about my parents and I'm still dealing with the big reveal of my heritage, along with the breakup, and now someone is blackmailing me.

I am *so* screwed. This is like a bad slasher movie. Some twisted version of I-Know-What-You-Did-Last-Summer. I clutch the warning message to my chest so Tanisha won't see it. Not that she's even paying attention because she is still rambling about going to the dentist.

"...then when I do it," Tanisha continues, flipping her dreadlocks over one shoulder. "The dentist claims he lost the barbell during my teeth cleaning. But I think my mom put him up to it. So can I borrow them tomorrow?"

Images flash through my mind like an erratic slideshow, displaying everything bad that'll happen if my secrets are revealed, like Sector Thirteen soldiers storming my house, and next comes the painful ice pick lobotomy, followed by my dad being sent to prison. My family will be ripped apart...

"Sloane?" Tanisha touches my shoulder. "Are you okay? You look like you're gonna spew chunks."

"Huh? Yeah, I'm good." I thrust the note into a pocket of my backpack and zip it tight.

Tanisha stares at me. "So can I or not?"

For the life of me, I can't remember what she wanted.

Oh, right—math class. And something about notes.

If someone at school knows my dark secret, taking notes in trig will be the least of my worries.

But I can't very well lose my mind in the hallway, so I force a stiff-lipped smile. "Uh-huh. I'll give you the notes tomorrow."

"Thanks! I gotta take off now. See you later."

Once Tanisha walks away, I inspect the corridor. My mouth goes dry. Whoever left me this warning might be skulking nearby, watching my reaction. My squinty gaze flits over each student lingering in the corridor, searching their expressions for any signs of guilt.

Emma Fowler and Kaitlyn Carter are gossiping at their lockers, and when they catch me staring, my frenemies glare. The culprit could be Emma. My friend Raymond McGregor walks by with a classic chin jerk to say hello, but he doesn't stop. A pack of giggling freshmen amble by, giving me a weird look. Hayden's younger brother, Zach Lancaster, stands at the other end of the hall, talking with one of his basketball teammates with his back to me.

Yet it suddenly seems as if the entire population of Haven High knows the truth....

***

Deep POV can make the story more interactive and intimate. Showing allows readers to experience differing emotions or visit exotic places. And a reader who feels like they're connected and really experiencing the story, is a reader who won't be able to put the book down.

SHALLOW: CURIOSITY

Quote: "If, however, you want to write a character from the ground up, a character who is as *real* as any person living, yet wholly your own creation, then there are three aspects you need to know in depth: the physical, sociological and psychological."—*Moody Writing blog, mooderino*

A curious character is one that might be super nosey or just naturally inquisitive. This type of character can constantly question other character's motives and inquire about certain situations. But it could also lead to them sticking their nose where it doesn't belong and causing wonderfully delicious conflict within the storyline. It is this overwhelming desire to investigate and explore that can motivate a character to solve a crime or uncover a mystery.

Having your character wonder about things is a great way to explore their thoughts and feelings within the storyline.

Curiosity can be a positive character trait or a negative one, depending on the storyline. An inquisitive character might be more adventurous and unafraid to venture into dangerous situations. For instance, a detective who's instinctively curious will catch the bad-guy, and an inquisitive teenage girl will figure out who stole the school mascot. And possibly, one of the most recognized character tropes is the nosy neighbor, which I think can be a fun personality to include in any type of genre.

Curiosity can also be associated with *wondering, speculating, questioning, snooping,* or *prying.*

Signs of curiosity might be:

Head tilting to the side

Raised eyebrows

Eyes big and round

Slowly nodding

Gesturing with hand for someone to continue speaking

Eyebrows creasing

Staring intently

Eavesdropping

Increased awareness of sensory information

Fidgeting or restless

Examples on how to revise shallow writing:

SHALLOW: I was curious what Ed and Mary were discussing in the next room.

DEEP POV: I crept closer to wall and pressed my ear against the wood. I *had* to know if Ed and Mary were talking about me.

SHALLOW: Tom was an inquisitive person.

DEEP POV: When I caught Tom rifling through my trash can to see what type of wine I drank, I knew it was time to move.

SHALLOW: Mandy was an odd and nosey person.

DEEP POV: Mandy asked a million questions while peeking into my dresser drawers.

SHALLOW: His constant prying had become annoying.

DEEP POV: Whenever anyone stopped by my house, my nosey neighbor would show up and casually ask me who had just left.

SHALLOW: He was curious about the monkey

DEEP POV: His gaze tracked the monkey swinging from the trees, waiting to see what he would do next.

SHALLOW: Her curiosity was an intricate part of her exasperating personality.

DEEP POV: Even as a child, Alice was always peeking into closets and rummaging through boxes in the attic.

SHALLOW: She was curious what he was thinking about.

DEEP POV: His stoic expression left no hint as to what he was thinking.

SHALLOW: I was curious about Melvin's whereabouts.

DEEP POV: I had no idea what Melvin was up to, but I was going to find out!

***

Here are two longer scenes illustrating how writers can avoid shallow writing and apply a Deeper POV. (In the first example, I underlined the shallower writing and any overwriting that is not needed.)

Please carefully examine these examples...

SHALLOW:

Harper did not know why her friend had suddenly returned.

"Do you know why Ella is back?" Aiden asked <u>Harper inquiringly.</u>

Why had my former best friend, Ella returned after inexplicably disappearing twelve months ago? Harper <u>wondered with curiosity.</u>

"Maybe she was abducted by aliens," Aiden <u>mused out loud.</u>

Harper ignored Aiden's absurd speculations. Ella was too pretty and amiable to ever join a cult or kill anyone, Harper <u>thought.</u> Harper even had to do all the dissecting in high school Biology because Ella couldn't bring herself to hurt the poor frog. But she was <u>dying of curiosity</u> (cliché), and it was fun to speculate.

"Harper, do you have any idea why Ella came back to town or not?" Aiden asked <u>Harper again in a questioning tone.</u> "Please tell me about your theories because I'm very curious."

Harper stared at him with a <u>curious expression,</u> and <u>felt</u> her face blushing hotly. The truth was, she hadn't spoken to Ella in over a year. Maybe Ella really had turned into a brainwashed cult leader or spent the last year in a penitentiary, Ella <u>thought to herself.</u>

"I have no idea," she said softly, and then added <u>inquisitively</u>, "But I'm curious to find out…"

The next version has been rewritten with more "voice," Deep POV, and more characterization.

DEEP POV:

"Hey, Harper, any idea why Ella suddenly came back to town?" Aiden wiggled his eyebrows. "Maybe she's been in jail for something like murder!"

She shook her head. Ella, her former best friend, had returned after mysteriously skipping town a year ago. Ella was too smart to ever join a cult or murder anyone. Harper smiled, remembering how she'd even done all the slicing and dicing in Biology because Ella couldn't bring herself to dissect the stupid frog.

Tilting her head, Harper tapped a finger on her chin. "I haven't got a damn clue."

"But it's weird, right?" Aiden scratched his curly head. "You must have a theory."

Harper blinked, and her oval face flushed hotly. For all she knew, Ella really had turned into a brainwashed cult leader or been locked up in some woman's insane asylum.

"Yeah, it *is* strange," she said, rubbing her chin. "But don't worry, I'll find out…"

***

By giving your characters realistic emotions and reactions, it gives them even more complexity. And being able to describe those emotions through Deeper POV adds mastery to your writing.

SHALLOW: RELAX

Quote: "One of the most common characterization mistakes writers make is granting their characters too much self-awareness. That sly pitfall puts tension at risk, limits believability, and inhibits the ability to *show* rather than *tell*." —*fiction coach, editor, and writer, MJ Bush*

To avoid stating the character's emotional state, like he/she relaxed, a writer can *show* a character taking a breather or loosening up in slower, reflective scenes.

Relaxing is a physical response to a lot of different emotions or events. For instance, if the character was almost caught stealing, but then managed to allude the cops, they would relax or calm down.

If the character had been tense or worrying about something, once it was resolved, they might visibly relax their posture or the stiffness in their shoulders.

Or if the character is feeling relieved after a strange turn of events within the storyline, and the writer wants to give the character a short reprieve before ramping up the action or tension again, they could show them unwinding.

Some physical signs of relaxing might be:

Breathing becomes slow and deep

Muscles become less tense

Yawning and stretching

Cracking the neck

Torso sags slightly to one side

Shoulders are not tensed up

Limbs hang loosely

Legs casually flung out

Putting hands behind head

Forehead lines un-creased

Examples on how to revise shallow writing:

SHALLOW: I saw my dad trying to relax before saying, "Okay. Tell me everything."

DEEP POV: My dad stretched out his arms, then let them drop. "Okay. Tell me *everything*."

SHALLOW: Tommy felt nervous, but then he relaxed. "It wasn't me. Honest," he said mildly.

DEEP POV: Tommy shook out his hands and kept his voice steady. "It wasn't me. Honest."

SHALLOW: I felt tense and I decided to try to relax.

DEEP POV: Tension stiffened my posture and made my jaw tight. I rolled my shoulders, trying to draw the stress away from my muscles.

SHALLOW: Trent wanted to relax, but it was difficult until he exhaled.

DEEP POV: Trent held in a breath, and then slowly released it.

SHALLOW: I felt determined to relax my body.

DEEP POV: I forced myself to unclench my fists.

SHALLOW: Lydia felt wound up and upset, but she needed to relax.

DEEP POV: Lydia pushed the air from her lungs, and the tension left her body.

SHALLOW: I wanted to ease the tension and calm down.

DEEP POV: I took a few deep breaths to steady myself.

SHALLOW: She forced herself to release the tension in her chest.

DEEP POV: She lowered eyelashes, and she let the breath swoosh from her lungs.

SHALLOW: I couldn't relax until I knew I was safe.

DEEP POV: Breath returned to me in a rush. I was finally safe.

SHALLOW: She decided to throw in the towel (cliché) as she said wearily, "Just bite my neck, Edward."

DEEP POV: Her shoulders sagged, her voice soft. "Just bite my neck, Edward."

Here are two longer scenes that illustrate how to avoid shallower writing and embrace a Deeper POV. (I have underlined what I consider to be shallower writing.)

Please closely analyze these two very different scenes…

SHALLOW:

"I need to find and kill that warlock," I said gravelly because I could not relax. "He might hurt my grandfather."

I saw my brother Peter visibly relax and I felt him wrap his arms around my shoulders. "I think you are ready to fight the warlock. Please try to be careful, sister," he whispered softly, then I saw him sped off down the hall.

I felt my body unwind as I watched him go into the kitchen. I turned to Ryan and breathed a sigh of relief. (cliché)

"Are you ready?" I asked Ryan honestly.

I saw him hold out his hand and I took it. I felt him squeeze it gently. "It'll be okay," he reassured calmly, but I didn't believe him.

I looked around me at the room, at how empty the living room was and felt a little disappointed when I realized that my best friend hadn't shown up yet. I'd texted her the night before, but I realized she thought that there was no reason to say goodbye to someone who was going to risk her life to fight a warlock.

I looked into Ryan's blue eyes. "She didn't come to say farewell," I told him matter-of-factly.

"No, she didn't," he stated truthfully. "But I am here."

"I guess there is no need to wait. I will right back," I <u>told him</u> and <u>headed</u> toward my grandfather's office.

DEEP POV:

"I *need* to kill that warlock." My posture stiffened "Before he tries to hurt Grandpa."

"Yes, yes. I agree. You're ready to face your enemy." My brother Peter rolled his shoulders, then wrapped his arms around me in a quick hug. "Please try to be careful, Sis," he whispered, then sped off down the hall and into the kitchen.

I blew out a breath and the tension in my body lessened. I turned to Ryan and slightly smiled. "Ready to do this?"

He nodded, then took my hand, and squeezed it gently. "It'll be okay."

But I didn't believe him. Fighting a warlock to protect my family was high up on the crazy scale.

My gaze swept over the empty living room and my stomach dropped. My best friend hadn't shown up. I'd texted her the night before, but maybe saying goodbye to someone who was going to fight a warlock was too hard.

I gazed into Ryan's blue eyes, then pulled my hand free of his. "She didn't come to say goodbye," I said, lowering my head and kicking at the ground with my scuffed combat boot.

He shrugged. "No, she didn't…but *I'm* here."

"Guess there's no need to wait. I'll right back." I marched out the door with my head held high and entered my grandfather's office.

***

Just remember that anytime a writer can remove the sensory "tell" from a scene and clearly describe whatever it is the character *saw* or *felt* or *tasted* or *heard* or *smelled*, it will automatically enhance the reading experience for the audience.

RHETORICAL QUESTIONS

Quote: "Deep POV is simply a technique that strips the author voice completely out of the prose. There is no author intrusion, so we are left only with the characters. The reader is nice and snuggly in the "head" of the character." —*editor and author, Kristen Lamb*

If Deep POV is done well, then the thoughts, emotions, moods, and experiences of the character(s) are interweaved so invisibly into the scene that the reader can almost experience everything along with the narrator, rather than having it itemized or stated for them. But much too often whenever a writer wants to express some kind of emotion, like confusion in their characters or add tension to a scene, they will include several rhetorical questions.

While a rhetorical question can focus on a particular character's inner-struggles, it should not be used instead of actually *showing* the characters' emotions and/or reactions.

Rhetorical questions shouldn't be used as a substitution for internal-dialogue or as the primary method for getting inside a character's head. There are much more effective and subtle ways to reveal a character's reaction or wonderment about an event or conversation, rather than using an internal question.

When I critique a novice writer's work, I often find that when they want to express some kind of uncertainty or curiosity or self-doubt in a character, they will overuse rhetorical questions. These interrogatory instances are a shallow way of establishing tension, and letting the reader know an internal debate is taking place by stating the obvious. The problem is that the misuse of rhetorical questions can become intrusive if the character asks multiple questions on the same page, or every time the author wants the reader to question something along with the narrator, which can become blatantly repetitive.

While rhetorical questions can raise tension, only use them if necessary when you cannot describe the reaction any other way.

Basically, a rhetorical question can be a way of *telling*.

Here are a few examples that should help you revise your own writing…

SHALLOW: I looked at my best friend with anxiousness. Why was Mary so mad at me? What had I done?

DEEP POV: I stared at my BFF and chewed on my lip. For the life of me, I couldn't understand why Mary was so pissed. I hadn't done a damn thing!

SHALLOW: Kent went down the stairs and into the basement and looked around the room that was dimly lit. What was Harold doing in the basement? Kent wondered.

DEEP POV: Kent crept to the bottom step of the basement stairwell and squinted into the dimness. Harold was up to *something* and Kent was going to figure out what.

SHALLOW: I went into the house very late past my curfew. Would my mom be waiting up for me? Would I be grounded for a month? I wondered.

DEEP POV: I snuck toward the house with my heart thumping. It was *way* past my curfew. If my mom was waiting up, then I was gonna be grounded for a month!

SHALLOW: She'd told the wizard that she only needed one wish, but he insisted on giving her three. *Why would he do that? Was this some type of trick?* Rainbow pondered to herself. *What would she do with three wishes now?*

DEEP POV: Rainbow scratched her head. She now had three wishes to use instead only one. Yet she wasn't sure if that was a good thing or bad. Or if it was some type of wizardly trick.

I have included a few longer examples to further illustrate this point. (In the shallow example, the questions are in italics.)

Please carefully examine these examples…

SHALLOW: I saw a ghostly shape in the doorway. I tried to hold back a silent scream as I stepped backward. *Why was there paranormal activity going on in my new home? Was I being haunted by a ghost?*

DEEP POV: A ghost floated in the doorway. With a silent scream stuck in my throat, I backed up into the wall. Okay, so there was some *obvious* paranormal activity going on in my new home.

Please carefully examine these examples…

SHALLOW: Brooks had asked me a lot of dumb questions on our first date. *Where better for an interior decorator to live than in one the most high-class cities in the United States? And what is it about guys that made them give the coldshoulder to a woman who says that she likes to wander around bookstores? Doesn't anyone like to read anymore?* Then he doesn't even ask me out again! *Why even ask about my hobbies if he wasn't interested in dating me?*

DEEP POV: I rolled my eyes and took another sip of wine. My first date with Brooks hadn't gone as well as I'd hoped. All those dumb questions about why I had moved to the city, and about my hobbies, and then snubbing me for being an avid reader.

I still wasn't sure what the point of asking me all those questions was—if the jerk wasn't even interested in a second date!

***

Too many rhetorical questions can deflate the tension of the moment. Writers should revise them whenever possible so that they are not in the form of a question. One clever way to do that is, if there two or more characters in a scene, then revise some of the inner-questions into actual dialogue. And it's an awesome way to add tension and create turn-paging prose!

Please carefully examine these examples…

SHALLOW: Damon shook his head. He deliberated to himself as he put down his keys angrily on the table. *Why was Jane so insistent on going to dinner tonight? Didn't she understand that he was exhausted after a long day at work? Would it be too much to ask for Jane to think about his needs first for a change?*

DEEP POV: Damon threw his keys down onto the table with a loud *clang*. He was being ambushed by Jane again.

"Damn it, Jane! Why are you so insistent on going to dinner tonight? Don't you understand that I'm exhausted after a long day at work?" Damon shook his head. "Would it be too much to ask that you put my needs first for a change?"

***

Were the examples helpful?

Have you read a story were the author endlessly pestered the reader with internal questions laced throughout the narrative like an interrogator?

Or writers who are trying too hard to show doubt about something that happens or they question another character's motives?

Or even strive to be funny or colloquial by using lots of inner-questions? Or breaking the tension by inserting questions every couple of paragraphs?

Were all those questions above getting redundant?

Of course, they're annoying!

Prose littered with rhetorical questions can be really irritating for the reader. Consider it this way: inner-questions are not *real* questions, but rather a way to "tell" the reader what the character's thought process is in the form of a question.

The exception to this guideline is when a writer wants to indicate sarcasm or humor. A few rhetorical questions laced into the narrative can really enhance a scene and strengthen a humorous "voice" when needed. And it can even be a necessity in some scenes where any other type of sentence just wouldn't fit the moment.

There are no hard-and-fast rules regarding where or even when it's appropriate to use a rhetorical question in your narrative. But it becomes rather clear when it's one of the instances of *telling* rather than actually "showing."

Experienced writers should understand that you need to do both, so I'm not stating that all rhetorical questions are wrong, but in my opinion they should be used with caution. And definitely don't ask more than two rhetorical questions on the same page.

If you limit the use of internal questions and only include them on occasion, then it's just another tool for your fiction writing toolbox.

Now I challenge writers to consider revising almost every question into *showing* a character's doubt, confusion, unease, etc., or turn it into actual dialogue whenever possible.

EMOTION: ANXIETY

Quote: "An author should know their character intimately, they should know their history, how they would react in any situation, they should know their look and mannerisms down to the smallest facial tick." —*author and blogger, Aaron Miles*

The easiest way to convey to a reader, without *stating the emotion*, whenever a character is feeling nervous or anxious, is to describe the character's body language. Since describing the body's movements and gestures can show readers what a character is feeling, it is often worthwhile to stay in Deeper POV.

For example, a character that is feeling anxious or worried might be described as defensive because they are subconsciously protecting themselves. Or a writer can *show* a character who's tense or apprehensive sitting on the edge of a seat, along with rapid foot tapping. Shifting weight from foot-to-foot or constant movement can describe a character that appears uncomfortable without stating it.

A nervous or anxious character might make bad decisions or cause tension for the hero. For this type of character, anxiety might not just be an isolated emotion, but rather a whole collection of real or imagined fears. The character might overreact because they perceive a threat, causing a fight-or-flight stress reaction.

Some physical signs of apprehension might be:

Men stand with their hands clutched in front of their genitals

Women fold their arms across their chest

Increased heart rate

Inability to breathe deeply

Tugging at collar

Rigid muscles

Clenched jaw

Restless / unable to sit still

Sweaty Palms

Trembling hands

Examples on how to revise shallow writing:

SHALLOW: I felt nervous going to the party alone.

DEEP POV: My jaw clenched as I neared the door of the party. *Man, I hated going places alone.*

SHALLOW: He hated confrontations and he was anxious to face Adam.

DEEP POV: Rolling his neck and shoulders, he faced Adam.

SHALLOW: "Where is Becky?" I asked nervously.

DEEP POV: "W-where is *Bbb*ecky?" I stammered.

SHALLOW: She was agitated and angry that he came home so late.

DEEP POV: She stood with her arms crossed and her foot tapping. "Where the hell have you been?" she demanded.

SHALLOW: I was feeling anxious about the long drive home on the winding road.

DEEP POV: My fingers gripped the steering wheel tightly, my gaze glued to windy road.

SHALLOW: Manny was flustered while waiting for his wife to give birth.

DEEP POV: Manny was jiggling his keys and pacing the hospital waiting room.

SHALLOW: I felt apprehensive and fearful about giving the speech.

DEEP POV: Shaking out my hands and arms, I cleared my throat several times and said, "Hello, I'm Daisy Price…"

SHALLOW: Mercy was rattled and she looked agitated.

DEEP POV: Mercy clutched her handbag to her chest like a shield.

SHALLOW: I feel apprehensive.

DEEP POV: My mouth went dry and my hands were trembling.

SHALLOW: He felt very uneasy and restless today.

DEEP POV: With sweaty hands, he tugged at his collar.

I have included a few longer examples to further illustrate my point. The first is written in Shallow POV with too many "ly" adverbs tacked onto the dialogue tags, and the speech is lacking "voice." (I have underlined what I consider to be shallower writing in the first example.)

Please carefully examine these scenes…

SHALLOW (info-dump):

"Do you have any questions?" Lily asked, <u>feeling apprehensive</u>.

The place in the forest where they'd followed the werewolves <u>felt cold and damp</u>. She <u>noticed</u> an <u>intent look</u> on William's face.

"There are really werewolves? And other supernatural creatures?" William <u>asked nervously</u>.

Lily <u>nodded her head in agreement</u>, although she <u>felt anxious</u>. "Yes, Except for some paranormal things," she <u>said seriously</u>.

"You should not have followed us," Jack <u>said sternly, wearing an angry expression</u>.

"Do you hunt werewolves?" William asked with <u>eagerness</u>.

"I only do when they attack innocent people," Jack <u>answered honestly</u>.

William <u>looked thoughtful</u> while contemplating how this news would change his world. <u>This is weird, he thought</u>. But so cool.

Lily was <u>worried</u>. She leaned forward <u>anxiously</u>, and touched William's hand. "Is this information upsetting you?"

"That is marvelous," he said with a <u>glimmer of excitement in his eyes</u>.

Jack looked startled. "Did you say marvelous?"

William nodded enthusiastically and it made the dark hair move on his forehead. He was delighted to know that paranormal creatures were real. "Yes, I did. It's like Supernatural, but *real*."

Jack felt nervous and anxious by William's response. "What are you talking about?"

"That is a TV show," Lily explained. She felt embarrassed. "On the TV show they mention a lot of paranormal occurrences."

Jack looked stupefied.

William grinned with amusement. "You've never heard of Supernatural?"

"I have heard the word supernatural," Jack said thoughtfully. "And vampires, however, they have mostly died out."

William looked disappointed. "Vampires are extinct? That is too bad."

Wasn't that tedious and boring to read? Why, yes. Yes, it was!

Now this second example has been revised into Deeper POV. The scene includes a few of the five senses and "voice" both in the dialogue and internal-thoughts, along with descriptive details.

DEEP POV:

Lily chewed on her bottom lip. "Any questions?"

The cave in the forest where they'd tracked the werewolves had damp walls and an eerie coldness that seemed to penetrate her heavy jacket. She shivered and moved closer to Jack. At least the mutts had vacated their den for the night.

Jack sighed. "*He* shouldn't have followed us here."

"Why not?" William's eyes grew wide. "Are there *really* werewolves? Demons, witches, and other supernatural creatures?"

Lily scratched her head, then slowly nodded. "All true. Except for trolls and unicorns. Those are myths."

"So, you hunt werewolves?" William turned to Lily's new boyfriend Jack and a goofy smile spread his lips. "Like it's your job?"

Jack laced his fingers behind his head and leaned back on his heels. "Yes, but only when they attack people."

William grew quiet and stared down at his feet. A chilly wind swept through the space, stirring up the pine needles. A pair of fireflies danced at the mouth of the cave.

Lily leaned forward, and lightly touched William's hand. "Are you okay? I mean, are you freaking out?"

William lifted his head and a slow grin overtook his features. "No...this is *awesome*."

The dark lashes gracing Jack's cheeks flew up. "Did you say awesome?"

Rubbing his hands together, William nodded, making the dark hair bounce on his forehead. "Yup. It's like Supernatural, but *real*."

The lines crisscrossing Jack's forehead deepened. "What are you talking about?"

"That's a TV show." Lily's face colored fiercely. "On the series, there are hunters and it has a lot of monsters, like vampires."

Jack just stared at William.

William grinned. "You've never heard of Supernatural?"

"I've heard of the word *supernatural*," Jack said in a serious tone. "And vampires. Even though, they've mostly died out."

William's smile drooped. "Vampires are extinct? That *sucks*. No pun intended…"

***

Just remind yourself that *showing* respects the reader's intelligence, and *telling* assumes that the reader is not clever enough to recognize the emotion or reaction unless the writer blatantly states it for them.

EMOTION: PANIC

Quote: "Basically, a panic attack is triggered by a thought. The thought itself could be originated by a variety of things, either it could come out of the blue, be a response to an outside stimuli or result from a long reflection..." —*Alex, Reference for Writers blog*

Panic is closely related to the emotion fear, and it also ties into worry or anxiousness. It is an emotion that brings upon a sudden sensation of terror or dread so strong that it can dominate or prevent rational thinking and cause overwhelming feelings of apprehension.

The important thing about writing any type of fiction is to always draw the reader deeply into the scene by relying on the POV character's senses and descriptions to paint a detailed picture, as though the reader is deeply experiencing everything right alongside the narrator.

If a character is having "panic attacks," it can add an extra layer of characterization to your story. When a character is experiencing a panic attack, it is common to feel their heart pounding, sweating, hyperventilating, chest pain, shortness of breath, nausea, tunnel vision, body shaking, etc. A character can become frozen and unable to move or react, or even defend themselves. Using short, choppy sentences to describe panic might work best.

Some physical signs of panic might be:

Tension in neck, back, shoulders

Unable to sit still

Crossed arms

Breathing faster and shallower

Clearing Throat

Trembling hands

Sweating

Bug-eyed

Mouth freezes / unable to speak

Pupils are small and un-dilated

Examples on how to revise shallow writing:

SHALLOW: I felt panicked.

DEEP POV: My stomach felt queasy and my hands wouldn't stop shaking.

SHALLOW: He was unnerved by the baby crying.

DEEP POV: With quivering hands, he lifted the wailing baby from the crib.

SHALLOW: I felt really flustered this morning.

DEEP POV: My breath became fast and shallow.

SHALLOW: When he saw the huge phone bill, he panicked.

DEEP POV: The phone bill crinkled in his sweaty fist.

SHALLOW: I felt panicky when Tom asked me to lunch.

DEEP POV: Big knots formed in my stomach.

SHALLOW: I felt unnerved.

DEEP POV: My insides felt like jelly.

SHALLOW: I felt a bout of panic. How could I pay my bills this month?

DEEP POV: Clutching collar of my shirt, I stared at the zeros on my bank statement.

SHALLOW: I felt like a nervous wreck. (Cliché)

DEEP POV: My mouth went dry and I couldn't sit still.

SHALLOW: I was feeling overly anxious.

DEEP POV: I wanted to run out the nearest exit.

***

Here are two longer examples of *showing* panic instead of stating it for the reader taken from one of my short stories.

The first scene has too much shallow writing, and the scene is lacking any "voice" or sensory details. (I have underlined what I consider to be shallower writing.)

Please carefully examine these two examples...

SHALLOW:

When I opened my eyes, I noticed it was still dark in the room. Feeling half-asleep, I got out of bed and headed into the bathroom. It must be late, I thought to myself. We had been on the run from the mobsters for three days and I felt very exhausted. Then I looked in the mirror. At first, I didn't recognize the face I saw reflected in it. I felt a headache come upon me. After washing my hands, I looked in the cabinet for aspirin, but I realized there wasn't any inside. So I left the bathroom, but then I stopped in the middle of the bedroom.

An unsettling feeling of panic welled inside me. I realized that something wrong, but I couldn't quite decide what it was. The atmosphere felt really strange. Anxiety was building up within me.

Suddenly, I realized what it was when I looked at the bed. I realized that my friend Elena was no longer in the room. I turned on the light and looked around the room. I noticed that her purse and shoes were gone.

I felt terrified. I looked at my watch and saw that it was almost midnight. *Where had she have gone at this hour? Why hadn't she told me that she was leaving? Why had she left me alone in a hotel room? When would she return? Should I call her cell phone?*

Now I felt really alarmed and worried. Hastily, I put on my jacket, then my shoes. I went out the door in a blind panic. (cliché) I knew I had to catch her before the mobsters did.

This second scene is the final draft that was revised to *show* the reader that the character starts to panic without stating it, and includes more detailed descriptions and a deeper character POV.

DEEP POV:

A soft *click* awoke me. I blinked into the dimness of the stuffy room, the faint glow of the bedside clock glowed eerily in the darkness. A sharp throbbing spread across my forehead, and I winced.

I fumbled with the scratchy blankets and stumbled into the bathroom, where I caught my reflection in the mirror. Being on the run from bloodthirsty mobsters hadn't done much for my complexion. Bloodshot eyes rimmed with dark circles and ashen skin made the face reflected back at me almost unrecognizable.

Opening the cabinet, I searched for aspirin, but only found a small bar of scented soap and a bottle of shampoo. I shuffled back into the bedroom and glanced at the bed. Even before my mind registered the emptiness, I knew she wasn't lying there.

Flipping on the overhead light, I scanned the room. My mouth dried. I couldn't swallow.

I spotted a leather wallet peeking out from under the jumbled pile of clothes. Sweat prickled my underarms and down my back. I hurried to the closet and checked inside. My garments were pushed to the far side, leaving a gap where her clothes should have been.

Spinning on my heel, I yanked on my jacket, shoved my bare feet into shoes, and bolted from the room.

***

If you're a beginner writer working on your first manuscript, or if you're reading this book to gain more knowledge and insight on the topic, I implore you to start using Deeper POV in all of your stories. You've heard the saying, "Practice makes perfect," right? After you finished at least five drafts of your current work-in-progress (WIP), it is time to go back and revise those shallower areas.

EMOTION: DISGUST

Quote: "*Changers* are characters who alter in significant ways as a result of the events of your story. They learn something or grow into better or worse people, but by the end of the story they are not the same personalities they were in the beginning. Their change, in its various stages, is called the story's emotional arc." —*author, Nancy Kress, "Write Great Fiction: Characters, Emotion & Viewpoint"*

One way to add conflict to a story and provide a growth ARC is to have a character that is seeking the approval of a boss or a parent, but only receives disgusted condemnation. Or a character who is repulsed by another character's actions or behavior in any given situation can add a level of depth to the scene if it is shown.

Disgust is a negative feeling of aversion or disapproval at someone or something. While feeling disgust, a character might notice an increase in heart rate, higher blood pressure, and a decrease in skin temperature. The saliva is overproduced, which could trigger the urge for a character to spit at the object or even at the person that they feel disgusted with.

Writers should avoid just stating that a character felt a sick feeling of revulsion (cliché), loathing, or nausea, and instead reveal that the character feels disgust by their facial expressions and reactions. And instead of using a cliché like, *Ron looked at his son's messy room and recoiled in disgust,* I would describe the room with sensory details so that the readers can witness the revulsion for themselves.

Some physical signs of disgust might be:

Curl of upper lips

An open mouth, the tongue pushing slightly forward

Wrinkled nose

Narrowing eyes

Lip corners are drawn down and back

Rolling of eyes

Making guttural sounds like "ewww" or "ugh"

Shaking one's head while muttering

Hands up, backing away with a fake shiver

Eyebrows pinched together

Recoiling away

Examples on how to revise shallow writing:

SHALLOW: I thought what he was doing was disgusting.

DEEP POV: Shaking my head, I muttered, "That's super gross."

SHALLOW: Nathan was repulsed by the dead body.

DEEP POV: Nathan recoiled and wrinkled his nose when he saw the cadaver.

SHALLOW: I was sickened by the sight of rotting food.

DEEP POV: I covered my mouth and nose when I got a whiff of the rotting food in the sink.

SHALLOW: She wore an expression of contempt. (cliché)

DEEP POV: She scrunched her brows and tilted her head to the side.

SHALLOW: Ben looked contemptuous.

DEEP POV: Ben's lips curled upward into a sneer.

SHALLOW: Lacy thought Jack was abhorrent.

DEEP POV: Lacy's steely gaze bore into his face.

SHALLOW: I was repulsed by his actions.

DEEP POV: My mouth puckered. "*Ewww!* Don't eat that worm."

SHALLOW: Cami thought he was a crude man.

DEEP POV: Cami leaned back and rolled her eyes.

SHALLOW: I saw Cordelia give me a disgusted look because I was wearing my gym clothes.

DEEP POV: Cordelia lifted her nose in the air as if the sight of me in my gym clothes offended her.

***

I have included two lengthier examples of how a writer might show "disgust" rather than bluntly state it. (I have underlined what I consider to be shallower writing.)

Please carefully compare these examples…

SHALLOW:

"Are you really not going to finish eating your food?" Amelia <u>looked at</u> Madison <u>with revulsion</u>. "You are going to make yourself sick."

Madison <u>looked down</u> at all the food that was on the table in front of her. <u>There was</u> still a big amount of fatty foods besides what she'd already consumed. "Can you put this food outside for me because I feel sick?" she asked.

Then Amelia <u>noticed</u> her stand up and <u>head</u> into the bathroom.

Amelia took the plates and deposited them into the trash can. She <u>could hear</u> Amelia being sick in the bathroom, the flush of the toilet, and then <u>the sound</u> of her rinsing out her mouth. She <u>felt disgusted</u> by her friend's bad habit of forcing herself to vomit after a heavy meal.

DEEP POV:

"Really?" Amelia shook her dark head and flashed Madison a tight smile. "You're going to *scarf and barf* again?"

Madison glanced at the pile of carbs still left on her plate. Her stomach pitched and bile rose in her throat. "Can you please dump this junk? I can't stand to look at it." Madison scooted back her chair, ran for the bathroom, and slammed the door behind her.

Amelia grabbed the plates and threw the leftovers in the trash. Through the bathroom door, violent retching, the slurping flush of the toilet, and then the gargling of mouthwash penetrated the wood.

***

Just keep in mind while you're revising your manuscript that great storytelling should be a mix of both showing *and* telling.

EMOTION: GUILT

Quote: "Usually, we combine internal and external conflicts for a richer story. That means we have to understand how our characters approach and resolve conflict." —*novelist and blogger, Jami Gold*

Guilt and shame can be great motivators for a character's actions and reactions. It can cause a lot of conflict within the storyline if guilt makes a character withdraw from their friends and family. Shame can even cause a character to lie about their past, or hide an ugly truth. These emotions can even cause a character to be in serious denial over a situation or about another character. Usually a character who feels ashamed will lower their head and look downward to avoid direct eye contact.

Remorse and shame are often obsessive emotional traits or reactions that can weigh heavily on a person's subconscious. While guilt might provoke a more positive response in a character, particularly when he/she is seeking to mend a broken relationship or correct a mistake, feelings of shame emphasizes what might be immoral or dishonest within themselves. Shame would have a much more inward focus for the character, and make them feel poorly about themselves, instead of just the actions they should've taken.

These emotions can become a character flaw that ties in with a theme, like redemption. For resolution, a character feeling guilty over something can overcome the fatal flaw through a heartfelt apology, or begging forgiveness, or by righting a wrong.

Some physical signs of guilt might be:

Avoid eye contact

Fidget when confronted

Flushed face

Angry outbursts / Defensive remarks

Rubbing the back of neck

Shoulders drawing up, elbows tucking into the sides

Becoming unnaturally quiet or still

A quivering chin

Hunched shoulders

Stuttering when talking

Examples on how to revise shallow writing:

SHALLOW: I felt very guilty.

DEEP POV: A sting of warmth stirred within my heart.

SHALLOW: He was overwhelmed with guilt. (Cliché)

DEEP POV: His chin quivered. He had to tell her the truth.

SHALLOW: I was too ashamed to face him. (Cliché)

DEEP POV: I couldn't look him in the eye.

SHALLOW: Elijah felt remorseful.

DEEP POV: Elijah's face flushed as he tried to explain.

SHALLOW: I felt so much shame.

DEEP POV: My scalp prickled with heat and I turned away.

SHALLOW: She was repentant for her actions.

DEEP POV: She inwardly winced and wished she take those harsh words back.

SHALLOW: Shame engulfed me over what I'd done.

DEEP POV: Biting my lip, I hurried away with my head down.

SHALLOW: James felt regretful.

DEEP POV: He repeatedly swallowed, trying to find the right thing to say.

***

Here is an excerpt taken from my college romance novel SMASH INTO YOU that depicts the emotion "shame" that makes the main character feel defensive and lie to hide her dark past.

Please carefully examine this example…

DEEP POV:

"I just don't like you like *that*." I glanced away because this wasn't just one of my many lies. This was a lie that hurt the both of us. "I think you're a great guy, but you're just not my type and I need to focus on my studies."

"You're lying. Again."

My head snapped in his direction. "*What?* No, I'm not!"

"Please. Your eyes are darting all over the place and your words don't match what's coming out of your mouth."

Damn. He was too perceptive.

"You don't even know me, Cole. I meant what I said."

"You're just scared for some reason to explore whatever this is between us. Try being honest for once, Serena. I can tell you play a good game, but I can spot a liar from miles away, and you're clearly hiding something. They say the truth will set you free."

The truth. Who knew what that was anymore?

I wasn't sure if I could tell anyone the truth. Lying had become a vicious circle. Once a person started, it was hard to stop without spinning out of control. So I did the only other thing I was good at besides being a master manipulator—running away...

***

Try to stay away from using descriptive adjectives like angry or happy or sad or guilt that *tell* the reader the specific emotions of the character, and instead revise to stay in a Deeper POV.

EMOTION: RESENTMENT

Quote: "Even if you find the bad-guy generally repulsive, you need to be able to put yourself so thoroughly into his shoes while you're writing him that, just for those moments, you almost believe his slant [viewpoint] yourself." —*bestselling author, K. M. Weiland*

Resentment is typically a companion emotion to envy and jealousy, and also bitterness. Feelings of resentment can result in a combination of animosity, anger, or even hatred from a real or imagined wrong or insult. Resentment can be a great way to add an extra layer of tension to any scene, or it could be a character's fatal flaw.

Resentment is typically an indication of a weakness. The villain of your story could be harboring a deep resentment for your hero, or maybe it's your main character that has this fatal flaw to overcome. This emotion can have a very negative affect on your character and how he/she reacts to certain situations. As a fatal flaw, it can make envy churn through their veins. Bitterness taste like bile. And even stain their soul. Use this emotion to add another layer of depth to your character's personality or use it as a theme.

Some physical signs of resentment might be:

Speaking sarcastically

Eyes widening

Speaking in a demeaning way

Looking down or away

Furrowed brows

Bared teeth

Mouth slack

Posture stiff

Face reddens

Neck grows hot

Examples on how to revise shallow writing:

SHALLOW: "Not now!" he said cruelly and felt a deep resentment.

DEEP POV: His thin lips were pressed tight. His words slow and menacing, "I…said…not…now."

SHALLOW: Wendee sounded resentful when she asked for tea.

DEEP POV: Wendee picked lint off her sleeve. "What time is tea? You *did* remember to make tea didn't you, Willow?"

SHALLOW: He resented my promotion.

DEEP POV: His chin tilted defensively higher and he turned his head slightly away.

SHALLOW: She looked like she bore a grudge against me.

DEEP POV: Her cheeks puckered as if she'd tasted a sour lemon.

SHALLOW: I have hard feelings about losing the race.

DEEP POV: I forced a smile while I gritted my teeth.

SHALLOW: I could tell she felt bitter about the divorce.

DEEP POV: Whenever the topic came up about her divorce, she avoided my eyes.

***

Here are two scenes to further illustrate my point on the difference between *showing* vs. *telling* that should inspire your creative muse. (I have underlined what I consider to be shallower writing.)

Please carefully examine these examples…

SHALLOW:

I was supposed to get the lead role in the school play and not Avery Weinstein.

She walked onto the stage and I instantly resented her presence. I had no reason to hate her, but I did. I hated everything about the girl. I resented her curvy body and beautiful face, and because she was popular with the other boys at school.

My eyes turned green with envy as I stared at that girl who had stolen my part. I couldn't stand the sight of Avery.

"We're Romeo and Juliet," Avery said delicately. She was good, I thought resentfully. "And we'll love each other until we die."

It was time to rehearse the kissing scene. I saw Benjamin clumsily move toward her, but then I watched him trip and lose his balance.

"I love you, too, my Juliet," he said hoarsely as he fell forward into her body.

"I've got you." I heard Avery laugh, and then I saw her catch him before he fell.

Then I watched him kiss her mouth. It was a long kiss and I felt even more bitterness. I saw their arms go around each other and then I heard him groan into her mouth.

"Stop action," Sofia, the director, said loudly.

I had felt and seen the attraction between Benjamin and Avery and it made me feel sick with revulsion. I decided that they did not mind kissing in front of the cast. If there weren't so many people around, I would have told Avery how much I loathed her.

"What a fun time I am having," Avery said happily. "What did you think of my performance, London?" I saw her look right at me.

"You were great," I said bitterly.

Please study this next revised version with "voice" and sensory details.

DEEP POV:

I was supposed to get the lead role in the school play—*not* stuck-up Avery Weinstein!

She strutted onto the stage like a queen with her commercial white smile.

I had no reason to hate Avery, but every fiber of my being felt strung tight. I hated her long, pale hair, her big brown eyes, and her flawless acting abilities. And the fact that she had more boys hanging on her than any other girl in school.

I stared at that disgustingly pretty girl who'd stolen my part, with an ugly sneer. I lifted a strand of my stringy black hair and then eyeballed her shiny blond waves. Yeah, I wanted her to break a leg. *For real.*

"We're Romeo and Juliet," Avery said in a light, whimsical voice. Damn, she was good. "And we'll love each other until we die."

Time to rehearse the kiss. Benjamin staggered toward her, tripping over the laces of his untied boots and losing his balance.

"I love you, too, my Juliet," he said, stumbling into her.

"Whoa there!" Avery giggled, catching him and he steadied himself.

Then he kissed her passionately. The seconds ticked by. Their arms wound around each other and he groaned softly.

Can anyone say, awkward?

"Cut!" Sofia, the director, shouted.

Not too soon either. The sizzling chemistry between Benjamin and Avery was totally nauseating, and they obviously had no qualms about making out in front of the cast. If there weren't so many people around, I would've pretended to gag.

"That was fun!" Avery smiled, then her gaze fell upon me. "What do you think, London? Was I great, or what?"

"Yeah, you were, um, great," I said, but my voice sounded tainted with sourness.

***

By giving your characters tangible emotions and physical reactions like in the revised scene above, it gives the people inhabiting your story-world even more realism.

EMOTION: PARANOID

Quote: "Developing a character with genuine depth requires a focus on not just desire, but how the character deals with frustration of her desires, as well as her vulnerabilities, her secrets, and especially her contradictions. This development needs to be forged in scenes, the better to employ your intuition rather than your intellect." — *author, David Corbett*

Giving a character an internal fatal flaw, such as paranoia when using the *man vs. himself* plot device to overcome might be an interesting growth ARC. A paranoid character will do reckless and rash things. He/she will be distrustful and fearful, or even unreasonable.

Recognizing the fatal flaw (character weakness) reveals what the character's internal journey will be. It becomes a big part of the plot in terms of a character's internal growth ARC, which will clarify the external conflict as well in your manuscript.

Flaws provide depth and tension, create empathy, and make a character more *human*. If a character has no flaws or seems too perfect, then all the conflict in the story is someone else's fault, and your main character is just drifting through scenes as an observer, and not actually connected or being affected by anything that occurs.

The problem is, readers need to care about what happens to the main character(s), so including a fatal flaw is a great way to achieve this.

Some physical signs of paranoia might be:

Tight jaw

Grinding teeth

Darting eyes

Mouth twitches

Restlessness / Pacing

Hyper-Alert

Folding arms over chest and shaking head

Mumbling to themselves

A disheveled appearance

Racing heartbeat

Eyes big and wide

Examples on how to revise shallow writing:

SHALLOW: I felt very paranoid when I entered the cemetery.

DEEP POV: Dark imaginings filled my head, and I cast crazed looks around the graveyard.

SHALLOW: Aria's paranoia was getting worse and she didn't trust doctors.

DEEP POV: Shuddering uncontrollably, Aria pleads, "Please don't make me go in to the hospital."

SHALLOW: He spoke harshly and the tone made me feel even more paranoid.

DEEP POV: His voice didn't sharpen, but it had an undercurrent that made Julia's shoulders go up.

SHALLOW: I was paranoid and scared of the dark.

DEEP POV: I gritted my teeth and my gaze darted around the dark room.

SHALLOW: I felt paranoia every time I had to enter the police station.

DEEP POV: A creeping sensation inched its way across my arms as soon as I entered the building smarming with cops.

Here are two longer scenes to encourage writers to *dig deeper* with their descriptions and characterization. (In the shallow example, I did not underline the shallower writing, but please try to see if you can clearly identify it now that you're more aware of *showing* vs. *telling*.)

Please carefully examine these examples…

SHALLOW (reads like a boring info-dump):

Maybe I was just feeling paranoid, but I hated showering in public places like my college dorm. Everyone else in the bathroom seems to feel comfortable undressed in public except for me.

I saw an empty shower stall, I move quickly past the girls either partially dressed or naked and then I pull the curtain closed tight, and I get undressed, and then hang my clothes on the rack outside the stall by sticking out one arm from the curtain. I turn on the shower, feeling fearful. The water takes a very long to get hot, and while I'm standing in the stall, I'm feeling paranoid that someone will open the curtain and they will see my naked body.

The shower is small and I do not have enough room to move. When I turn my body as I wash my hair, my elbow touched the rack that my clothes are on, and the clothing falls to the wet bathroom floor.

"I cannot believe that I did that." I groan to myself, and shut the water off, and then wrap my towel around my body.

I grab my pile of wet clothes and then I leave the bathroom to walk down the corridor, and I hope no one sees me naked, but I feel paranoid that people are watching. I get to my room and open the door. As I push the door closed behind me, I see a tattooed, black haired young man sitting on my roommate's bed. This is very embarrassing for me and I feel myself blush.

Please study this next revised version with "voice" and sensory details.

DEEP POV:

Shuffling my feet, I trudge down the corridor toward the bathroom like an inmate on death row. Showering in my college dorm has always made my skin crawl. It's not about my body, but all the other bodies that were there before me. The need to let the water run blazing hot for ten minutes before I slid my flip-flops off and let my toes touch the floor is beyond OCD.

I hesitantly enter the humid space, clutching my toiletries firmly against my chest as my gaze scans the steamy room. Other girls are in differing arrays of dress, some half-naked while others walk around in just a thin towel. The combined odors of mildew and flowery shampoos assault my nose.

I spot an empty shower stall, and hurry into it, yanking the plastic curtain shut. With trembling fingers, I undress, and then lean out holding the curtain over my nakedness and hang my clothes on the rack. Quickly, I turn on the water, but it takes forever to get hot. The billowy steam helps to slightly ease my nerves.

Finally, in a cloud of steam, I'm able to speedily wash my hair. Just as I'm rinsing out the shampoo, my elbow pokes out of the curtain and hits the rack.

This. Cannot. Be. Happening. *It's like my worst fear come to life!*

Turning off the water, I dry off, and then peek out the curtain. My shirt, jeans, and underwear lay in a soggy heap on the wet floor.

"Dammit," I mutter.

I wrap the towel around my damp body. Leaning down, I snatch up my sodden clothes and make a mad dash back to my dorm room, holding the towel around me with one hand. I speed-walk like a racehorse galloping toward the finish line.

When I get to my room, I slam the door closed behind me, then slump against the wood and close my eyes. *Finally.*

Someone clears their throat. My eyes snap open, and a tattooed, black haired guy sitting on my roommate's bed waves hello.

I want to die. *Now.*

***

Did you compare the last two examples? Are you starting to grasp how shallow writing pulls the reader out of the story?

Naming the emotion is a bad habit that writers easily fall into, which focuses the story on *telling* rather than *showing*. But Deep POV can turn a dull scene into one that remains in a reader's thoughts long after the book has been read. So please don't just state how a character feels, but try to make the reader actually feel it, too.

CONCLUSION

Quote: "The bestselling writers who endured fifty, or even a hundred rejections, before finally achieving success would make for such a long list of names that I would develop carpal tunnel syndrome just typing them all. Perseverance is as important as talent and craftsmanship." —*bestselling author, Dean Koontz*

Now that you have a clearer idea on how to revise shallow scenes by using the Deep POV technique, search for *telling* sentences and revise them by applying this amazing tool, but please avoid using overworked clichés in your writing.

Although, most books will probably offer similar advice about the Deep POV method, you can still gain the balance of study, theory, and practice that you might need to fully grasp these wonderful skills through additional reading. If you'd like to discover even more ways to strength your prose, I suggest studying these amazing books by this talented writers.

Recommended nonfiction reading:

"Rivet Your Readers with Deep Point of View" by Jill Elizabeth Nelson

"Mastering Showing vs. Telling in Your Fiction" by Marcy Kennedy

"The Emotion Thesaurus" by Angela Ackerman and Becca Puglisi

"Writing With Stardust" by Liam O' Flynn

"The Art of Description: Bring Settings to Life" by Anne Marble

"How to Write Dazzling Dialogue" by James Scott Bell

"Take Your Pants Off" by Libbie Hawker

***

And one of the best ways to learn and improve your own writing talents is by observing how other published writers do it. Go to your local library, bookstore, or favorite online retailer to purchase a few books to read in Deep POV.

Recommended fiction reading by these brilliant authors:

Kresley Cole

Brenna Yovanoff

Marjorie M. Liu

Jill Elizabeth Nelson

Well, that concludes my advice on self-editing filter words and how to revise your wonderful story into a Deeper POV that provides your readers with an amazing, unput-downable reading experience.

FINAL WORD OF ADVICE

Quote: "I love the rewriting and redrafting process. Once I have a first draft, I print the whole thing out and do the first pass with handwritten notes. I write all kinds of notes in the margins and scribble and cross things out. I note down new scenes that need writing, continuity issues, problems with characters and much more. That first pass usually takes a while. Then I go back and start a major rewrite based on those notes..." —*Joanna Penn, The Creative Penn blog*

If you've finished writing a novel or short story, then congratulations! That is a huge accomplishment to be very proud of, but now comes the revision work that will *really* make your story shine...

When I was growing up, the only thing I ever dreamed about was being a professional author. I realize for self-published and indie authors that it's an on-going struggle to get your books out into the world, and hopefully make some money in the process.

Like every writer, I am incredibly passionate about my work. The main reason I write is because I like to do it. Not for the money. No, because I love creating characters. I love crafting suspense. And I love telling stories—*my* kind of stories.

Best-selling author, Tracy Hickman was quoted as saying, "Don't seek to be published, seek to be read."

Simple words. Great advice. Write for your readers. Write what you love. Write every day and don't give up.

I've written a lot of books. Some good, and some, well, *not* so good. My first three novels were traditionally published without a literary agent. And I hate to tell you that the advance was dismal and I didn't sell as many books I'd hoped.

Looking back, I know what I did wrong. I didn't have any critique partners. The manuscript wasn't tightened up and polished enough. I didn't hire a professional, freelance editor.

A first or second draft should never, *ever* be what a writer self-publishes. As a matter of fact, the first draft or two should be ruthlessly edited. Personally, I do at least ten or more drafts on my own fiction stories.

Please do not rush to publish your book!

If you have a slower scene that readers might think is boring,' but you feel is vital to the plot, then find a way to Deepen the POV and the characterization, and also ramp up the tension.

Learn to self-edit if you can't afford to hire a professional editor. Find a few good critique partners (and if you don't know what this is, then that's a red flag that you might not be ready to self-publish yet), and really take the time to study story structure. I recommend that new writers read books in the genre that you want to write in and dissect them. Devour them. Analyze every aspect of the writing. Be patient and never stop improving your craft. As you write, and read, and study, you'll get better at including Deep POV in earlier drafts.

Once you've finished the fifth draft of your manuscript, then you're ready to use the Deep POV method. This is when you will go through each scene and find all the shallower writing and revise the heck of it.

As always, I wish everyone much success on their writing journey!

HUMBLE REQUEST

If you read this handbook and find the tools and tips helpful to improving your own storytelling abilities, please consider posting an honest review on Amazon, Barnes & Noble, or Goodreads. Word of mouth is crucial for any author's success, and reviews help to spread the book love. So please consider leaving a short (a sentence or two is fine!) review wherever you purchased this copy and/or on Good-reads.

If I get enough reviews stating that this guide helped writers to hone their craft, then I'd love to include additional books in this Deep POV series with new topics such as romance, suspense, and world-building.

And please visit my blog, "Fiction Writing Tools," for tons of helpful advice on book promotion, author branding, and self-editing.

BONUS MARKETING TIPS

Read on for a two more chapters filled with amazing tips on book promotion for self-published authors from my inspiring guidebook, which can double your sales within weeks!

HOW TO INCREASE YOUR BOOK SALES IN 30 DAYS

This in-depth marketing guide is perfect for writers publishing their first novel or indie authors trying to gain a wider readership. The manual includes valuable tips on networking, how to get more book reviews, and contains wonderful advice on how to best promote your work from established authors and popular book bloggers.

Whether you're a multi-published author looking to expand your audience or a self-published writer, this book will instantly give you the tools to market your fiction like a pro! Free bonus features include how successful authors use social media to connect with potential readers, reviewers, and how to sell more books.

BOOK PACKAGING

Great Tips on Book Cover Design that Self-Published Authors Need to Know!

Have you ever bought a book with a horrible cover from an author that you've never heard of?

I bet it's unlikely.

A stunning cover can attract a reader's attention and have them buying your eBook over the competition. It's like the first impression that a reader has of your wonderful product.

Most self-published authors and indie publishers use stock photos and images from sites such as CanStockPhoto or ShutterStock, etc. on their book covers. Even the bigger traditional publishers use stock images.

The only problem is that there are a lot of very popular models that are used repeatedly on book covers. Some photographers just have perfect models and poses that make stunning book cover designs, so they get used again and again.

Personally, I think stock images are great for book covers if you're a writer on a budget. And I see nothing wrong with using them.

From my professional experience, readers don't care, either. If it fits the genre, that's all that should matter. Just alter the image enough so it doesn't look exactly like the original stock photo.

However, I would make sure that your design is unique to your book when using the same stock image that's featured on someone else's cover. The key word is "unique" though, because it would be hard to find professional stock images that haven't already been used before.

The truth is, any stock photo can be used on another book cover. Stock photos/images can be licensed to thousands of different people who purchased the same one. To ensure that the images you picked out for your cover don't mirror someone else's design, I suggest altering the fonts, style, and colors effects, and including other elements to make your own book cover stand-out, and so that it doesn't look exactly the same as another author's design. It is almost unavoidable and just part of the publishing business. But no one wants to be labeled a copycat.

The first rule of packaging a product, and yes your book is a product, is attraction. Plus, branding. Think of Tiffany & Co. The recognizable light-blue box (branding) is more identifiable than the jewelry itself.

How a book is packaged may be what attracts the reader to take a closer look at the product (the novel.) Packaging (book covers) also play a very important role for portraying information about the product, like the genre.

A book cover (outer packaging) should have an attention-grabbing appearance. Your cover needs to be instantly recognizable within the genre that you write. Do lots of research and figure out where your book should be best placed within the market and what genres it fits. Study what works for bestsellers in a similar genres, after all, they're the authors you'll be competing with.

Don't worry if you find the same stock image being used on another book cover, unless the designs are too similar, then writers should alter their cover immediately.

My advice is to really take the time to learn about marketing and cover design. A book cover is just pretty packaging that hints about the story. The actual novel is what the reader is paying for, and I think some writers forget that. A book cover is only "packaging" for marketing purposes. What a writer wants on the cover doesn't mean it necessarily meets the expectations of what a potential reader might be looking for in a particular genre.

For instance, let's say that your book is a science fiction / steampunk novel, so you want a unicorn, and a floating hot-air balloon with your main character riding inside, along with circus monkeys and aliens on your cover because those are just a few of the awesome things that happen in your wonderful story, but will it make an eye-catching design?

Probably not.

Instead, I recommend visiting goodreads and Amazon to check out the bestsellers in the categories that your book falls under and study them! Then buy a premade cover or create a design that fits your genre.

Also, it is a general advertising principle that having a face and/or people on (a product) the cover will help to sell more books. The model doesn't need to look exactly like your hero or heroine, but just enough so the reader can form their own image of your characters in their mind.

All of the premade eBook covers on my own site, **SwoonWorthy Book Covers**, were designed in a wide range of genres for self-published and indie authors on a budget. (And these covers are also great for wattpad or fanfiction writers, too.) These inexpensive designs will give your work a professional look, so please browse each genre. Even if you feel like you can't afford a premade cover, I'm more than happy to work with authors on pricing. I have hundreds of book covers to choose from.

Even if you've already published a few books, or you're just starting out in the indie publishing world, there's always more to learn on the craft of fiction and book promotion. If you're determined to take your writing career seriously and make it to the next level, you need to make sure that your author branding and book packaging are "genre specific" to hit your target audience and build a loyal readership.

AUTHOR PROMOTION

First, let's chat about promoting your novel(s). The main hardship about being self-published or an Indie author is that you don't have a huge marketing department behind your work like most traditional authors do. The most important thing to remember is that, the minute you publish your first novel, you have become an entrepreneur. You have started your own business that revolves around *you* as the author (your brand) and your novel(s).

Most of my friends and family are not very supportive, so I cannot even count on them to buy my books. It's all up to me. I have become the writer, marketer, and promoter of all of my novels.

Many authors will advise newbies to keep writing books and skip the promoting, but I strongly disagree with that. If you don't do any marketing or request book reviews, then no one outside your family and friends will even know that you've published a book! If you want to turn this into a moneymaking career, then promotion is essential.

The day after one of my books is ready to be reviewed, I will spend about two months requesting book reviews and marketing my newest novel on a daily basis.

For about four to seven hours each day, I promote my newest novel on Twitter, my other social media sites like Facebook, and contact book bloggers about either featuring a guest post on their site or requesting a review. I have a huge contact list of over two thousand book reviewers that I can email and politely ask them to help market my novel.

If you've been in this industry for a while or you've just published your first book, I'm sure you've already realized by now that there is a ton of different ways to build a readership, obtain honest book reviews, and promote your fictional novel. If you want to achieve success, one important factor is getting books reviews. For most online retailers, getting reviews is crucial to getting your novel recognized by the website's recommendation algorithm. The best way to start is to contact book review bloggers and send them a request to read and review your novel.

Let's start with the basics, requesting someone to read and review your novel. There is a "write" way and a "wrong" way to approach book bloggers/reviewers about reading your work. It might be obvious to some of you, but I'll go over this step-by-step for those who don't know where to begin.

Knowing the genre and sub-genres of your novel is an important part of the first step and it will save you a lot of time. Do you write cozy mysteries? Dark and spooky horror? Light and fluffy contemporary romance?

If you're not sure what your genre is, just go online to places like Goodreads, Shelfari, Library Thing, Gnooks, or WhichBook and search for other authors whose writing style is close to your own. Visit the books page and read some of the reviews. (I don't recommend contacting readers or book reviewers through these sites and soliciting your novel or series. It is unprofessional and impolite. These are considered social forums to discuss literature. Instead, join some of the groups and discussions and if you make some new friends, then casually tell them about your novel.)

Step One:

Open up a browser on the Internet and search for book bloggers. Or find a list of possible reviewers separated by genre and listed alphabetically through helpful sites like the Book Blogger Directory.

One thing that might help narrow down your search is to look for book reviews of novels in your genre or other authors whose work is similar to yours. For instance, when I was seeking reviews for my adult novel, IMMORTAL ECLIPSE, I Googled "paranormal romance novel reviews." I also searched with keywords like "Gothic," "urban fantasy," and "dark romance." Be creative and use your keywords wisely. Then from that search, I contacted book reviewers who read and enjoyed the PNR (paranormal romance) genre.

There is no point in wasting your time or the reviewers by requesting a review from a blog that doesn't even read your genre. Most book bloggers clearly state on the "review policy" page of their site what type of genres they review and don't. Just move on.

There are thousands of book reviewers, so strive to find the ones that actually read your genre. You'll also get more positive reviews this way, then if you try to peddle your "science fiction space opera" novel to a book reviewer who only reads and reviews historical romance. Read posts on their site and some of their book reviews, and by doing this alone, you'll be able to tell if your novel is a good fit for their site.

Step Two:

Once you have found a site that reviews books in your genre, locate the "review policy" or "about" page on the site. Sometimes their policy is under the "contact" page, so you may have to look around. Read it *carefully*. Sometimes it'll state that they are not accepting review requests at this time. Again, I advise you to just move on.

Or if they are not accepting review requests, but they are offering to feature guest posts, you can send an email regarding a promo instead if you like.

Step Three:

Most reviewers will have either an email address or a contact form on their site.

Before you contact the reviewer, make sure to double-check the links in your book review request document. Make certain that you spell their name correctly. Include your email contact information, but do not include your home address or phone number. (This is not a job resume.)

The final step is to send off the request!

FICTION WRITING TOOLS

Bestselling author S. A. Soule shares her expertise with writers by providing surefire, simple methods of getting readers so emotionally invested in their stories that booklovers will be flipping the pages to find out what happens next.

Each of these helpful and inexpensive self-editing books in the *Fiction Writing Tools* series encompass many different topics such as, dialogue, exposition, internal-monologue, setting, and other editing techniques that will help you take your writing skills to the next level.

THE WRITER'S GUIDE TO CHARACTER EMOTION

Most writers struggle with writing a captivating story. The fastest way to take your writing to the next level is by the use of "Deep Point-of-View" which can transform any novel from mediocre storytelling into riveting prose. This manual will explain how you can greatly enhance your characterization, and how to emerge your readers so deeply into a scene that they'll experience the story along with your characters. Also, learn how to avoid "telling" by applying "showing" methods through powerful examples that will deepen the reader's experience through vivid, sensory details.

THE WRITER'S GUIDE TO VIVID SETTINGS AND CHARACTERS

Learn to Create a Realistic Setting with Atmospheric Detail and Lifelike Characters!

In this comprehensive writing fiction manual, you will learn how to create extraordinary worlds and deeply submerge your readers into the story. Constructing lifelike scenes isn't easy, unless you have the tools to write vibrant, authentic settings.

This manual also provides vital techniques on world-building with bonus examples on how to combine the five senses and use deep POV in all of your scenes. This valuable reference guide is useful in revealing a simplified way to create unique settings and vivid character descriptions flawlessly.

THE WRITER'S GUIDE TO AUTHENTIC DIALOGUE

A Powerful Reference Tool to Crafting Realistic Conversations in Fiction!

This manual is specifically for fiction writers who want to learn how to create riveting and compelling dialogue that propels the storyline and reveals character personality.

Writers will also learn how to weave emotion, description, and action into their dialogue heavy scenes. With a special section on how to instantly improve characterization through gripping conversations. All of these helpful writing tools will make your dialogue sparkle!

THE WRITER'S GUIDE TO PLOTTING A NOVEL

Awesome Tips on Crafting a Riveting "Hook" that instantly Grabs Your Reader

This manual offers amazing techniques for creating stronger beginnings and ways to write a page-turning "hook" for your fiction novel. Writers will learn how to make the first five pages so intriguing that the reader won't be able to put your book down, and reveal how you can successfully craft your first chapter.

Also, writers will get the tools needed to blend character goals with a riveting scene, and how basic plot structure can effectively and instantly strengthen the narrative. Plus, get bonus tips from other bestselling authors, advice on self-publishing a novel, and help with manuscript word counts. Whether you're writing an intense thriller or a sweeping romance, all novels follow the same basic outline described in detail within this book.

THE WRITER'S GUIDE TO BOOK BLURBS and QUERY LETTERS

An Awesome Book Description is One of the Most Important Tools a Writer Needs to Sell More Books, or to Gain the Attention of an Agent ...

Whether you're self-publishing, or querying agents and publishers, this guidebook on book descriptions can help! Writing back jacket copy (blurb or marketing copy) can give most writers a major headache. In this in-depth reference manual, any writer can learn how to instantly create an appealing blurb with a captivating tagline, or write a perfect query letter.

In this valuable resource, there are numerous query letters templates and book blurbs examples for almost every fiction genre that will have an agent asking for more, and/or help a self-published author to write a compelling product description that will boost their book sales.

HOW TO INCREASE YOUR BOOK SALES IN 30 DAYS

Learn How To Sell More Books in a Month!

This in-depth marketing guide is perfect for writers publishing their first novel or indie authors trying to gain a wider readership. The manual includes valuable tips on networking, how to get more book reviews, and contains wonderful advice on how to best promote your work from established authors and popular book bloggers.

Whether you're a multi-published author looking to expand your audience or a self-published writer, this book will instantly give you the tools to market your fiction like a pro! Free bonus features include how successful authors use social media to connect with potential readers, reviewers, and how to sell more books.

ABOUT THE AUTHOR

S. A. Soule is a bestselling author and Creativity Coach, who has years of experience working with successful novelists. Many of her fiction and non-fiction books have spent time on the bestseller lists.

Her handbooks in the "Fiction Writing Tools" series are a great resource for writers at any stage in their career, and they each offer helpful tips on how to instantly take your writing skills to the next level and successfully promote your books.

Please feel free to browse her blog, which has some great tips on creative writing online at: *Fiction Writing Tools* and visit her *Creativity Coaching Services* site for help with writing book blurbs, fiction editing, and revising your stories with Deep POV. And check out her inexpensive and awesome premade book covers at SwoonWorthy Book Covers.

Printed in Great Britain
by Amazon

Come Away,
O Human Child
and other tales

Ian Thomson

Published by The Quirinal Press

First published 2016

Copyright © Ian Thomson 2016

Come Away, O Human Child *was runner-up in the East Midlands Writers Competition in 1912*

and first published in the Lincolnshire Echo, August 2012 as The Piper.

These stories are entirely fictional and the characters in them are not

intended to represent anyone living or dead.

For My Sixth Form

Si la jeunesse savait; si la vieillesse
pouvait.

Voltaire

By the same author

The Mouse Triptych

The Swan Diptych

Hibernation

O what a tangled web we weave
When first we practise to deceive.

Sir   Walter
Scott

When he was about four, Lucas kept a kiwi fruit as a pet. He had made a kind of crib for it out of a tin which had contained Marks and Spencer's Curiously Strong Mints, and he had lined it with some cotton wool. The coverlet was a square of black fabric with the Specsavers logo on it that his father used to clean his glasses. When his dad wanted to reclaim it, Lucas wailed so piteously that his father said it was fine - he could easily get another one. Because his mother had told him that kiwi fruit are sometimes known as Chinese gooseberries, Lucas had named his pet Penghui, after a Chinese boy at school. The crib was kept on top of a radiator in Lucas's bedroom, despite his mother's protests, and he kept his bedroom curtains closed at all times so that Penghui should not be disturbed. Lucas's mother had protested about this too, but to no avail. Further tantrums had started to brew and she lacked the stamina to face them. This was a great shame, for Lucas's father had papered his room with an aeroplane design featuring Spitfires, Hawks, Vulcans and Lancaster bombers and now no-one ever got to see them. To be honest, Lucas had been pretty indifferent towards them from the start and it was more important that Penghui's sleep should not be disturbed by the light than anything else in the whole wide world.

In many ways, it was his mother's fault. She had picked up the kiwi fruit during her weekly shop as a treat for Lucas, who had never seen one. When she handed it to him, without explanation, he had asked if it was alive. Amused and charmed by the idea, she had said that it was hibernating. Lucas knew what this meant because his sister, Amber, had a tortoise called Nijinsky. She had grown bored with it long ago and it had been left to her mother to feed it fruit and cabbage stalks, which it would slowly devour with its horny, beak-like mouth. He was particularly partial to red grapes which he would tear apart, exposing the glistening purple flesh beneath the skin. Apart from that, he was left to wander the garden with his laborious overarm crawl. From to time, he would be lost in the shrubbery for a couple of days, but he would always reappear to continue his random patrol of the lawn and flowerbeds. Once, when she was about Lucas's age, Amber had picked Nijinsky up to kiss him and he had nipped her lip and then urinated down her white party frock. She had been disgusted by the dark brown stain on her white ballet dress and the spots of blood from her lip and their estrangement dated from then.

Lucas had been with his mother in the garden shed as she prepared a hibernation box for Nijinsky. It was made from two cardboard boxes, one inside the other, and the gaps between the big box and the smaller one had been filled with those polystyrene pellets you get from Amazon for fragile purchases. There were plenty of air holes. She explained to Lucas that the inner box was to limit Nijinsky's movements. A tortoise doesn't just sit in his hibernation box like a pie, she told him. He will attempt to move about and may even wake up and try to burrow through the insulation and out of the box into the outside world. If he succeeds, exposure to extreme cold could blind him. His eyes could quite literally freeze solid. Or even worse, the cold could kill him in no time. Lucas let out a wail and shot indoors and up to his room to check on Penghui.

It was fine. Penghui was safely asleep. In any case, there was no way he could possibly eat his way out of a tin. Carefully, he lifted his pet from the crib and, cradling it in the palm of one hand, he stroked it gently, enjoying the prickly fuzz. He had no idea why the grown ups called it a kiwi fruit when it was obviously an animal. Perhaps it was because it was a baby: it would grow up to be a kiwi, whatever that was. Grown-ups were funny. They never explained things properly. Gently, he returned Penghui to his crib. Spring was a long way away and he couldn't wait for the kiwi to wake up and become his playmate. He imagined that its head, legs and tail had retracted into the fuzzy body, like Nijinsky's, and that one sunny morning when the daffodils were in bloom, they would peep out. He thought a kiwi probably had four short, busy legs, a stubby little tail, and a head with little pointed ears, quivering whiskers, and a long snout with a button nose like a twitching currant. Lucas was certain that Penghui would be cute and frisky and nothing like boring old Nijinsky.

One dull morning in the middle of December, Lucas's mother was cleaning his room and took a look at the kiwi fruit. It was very soft underneath. She realised, with a pang of apprehension, that it would very soon start to rot and leak. Lucas would be devastated. There were two options open to her: she could tell Lucas the truth (she would have to one day, anyway, she now realised), or she could replace it. The truth was out of the question, for now anyway. He was so besotted with the thing that she hadn't the heart to tell him. It would be like telling a child that there was no Father Christmas. The other option was a nuisance but she would have to take it if there was to be peace in the household. Penghui would have to be replaced.

There was a problem, however. Close to the stem end of the kiwi fruit was a little black mark. It couldn't be ignored, for Lucas had explored every millimetre of his sleeping friend and declared to his mother that, when Penghui came out of hibernation, the little black mark would prove to be just over one of his eyes. Lucas was so sure of this that he was prepared to bet on it and in the end his mother found herself, contrary to common sense and with a vague sense of alarm, betting that the little black mark would be at the tail end and not just above one of Penghui's eyes. The stake was fifty pence.

So here she was, in the fruit and vegetable aisle at Waitrose, checking every kiwi fruit in the display to see if she could find one with a little black mark near the stem end. It was getting very close to Christmas and the store was packed. There is something about this time of year that makes it the very antithesis of the season of goodwill. Maybe it's to do with a spurious sense of urgency; maybe it's to do with a sense of guilt at the needless expenditure in the laden trolleys; maybe it's the long queues at the checkout, but shoppers in supermarkets tend to be irascible and impatient. As she examined each individual fruit and turned it over in her hands with the delicacy of a surgeon, she became aware of a man, standing nearby. Raising her eyes slightly, she saw both of his hands drumming impatiently on the handle of his trolley. She raised her eyes to look at his face.

'Any time before New Year,' he said.

He didn't look the type for kiwi fruit. Or persimmons, or cumquats or star fruit or lychees or mangosteens or any of the other exotic fruits that appear in supermarkets at this time of year. He didn't even look the type for Waitrose, she thought.

'It's for my son,' she said, realising even as she spoke, that this explained nothing. She smiled, thinly.

"Oh yes. And who would he be then? Baby Jesus?'

She looked down, offended and embarrassed, and noticed that the fruit she had just picked up had a little black mark near the stem end.

Her smile widened.

'And a very happy Christmas to you too,' she said and moved on serenely to look for chestnut stuffing and cranberry sauce, with Penghui II safely nestled among the tangerines in her trolley.

Lucas noticed nothing. He decorated the tin crib with tinsel and Christmas passed without tantrums or scenes.

Twice more, over the next month or so, Lucas's mother struck lucky in Waitrose. The winter had been very cold and the central heating in the house had had to be on full, day and night. Lucas refused point blank to have the crib anywhere but on the radiator, which was, of course, no place for a kiwi fruit. If she even touched it in his presence, Lucas's lower lip would begin trembling, sure sign of an impending screaming fit. However, one afternoon in late January, she drew a complete blank in her search for Penghui V. She had handled every kiwi fruit in the box on display without success. Every single one was annoyingly perfect. Fortunately, there were very few people in the store in the post-festal doldrums and she was not interrupted. She chose one anyway, miserably thinking that she would have to dream up some excuse for the absence of the mark which Lucas would believe.

When she had finished her weekly shop, she went to the stationery aisle to look for an amusing birthday card for Lucas's birthday, which was later in the week. As she browsed, her eyes lit casually on the pens nearby and then focused on the indelible marker pens. Would it work? She selected a black pen, ripped it excitedly from its packaging, removed the top, plucked the kiwi fruit from the trolley, and pressed the pen against the fuzzy, green-brown skin at the stem end. It was perfection. The little black indentation looked indisputably organic. Lucas would never know the difference and, what is more, her humiliating searches through the kiwi fruit stocks were over for good. She let out an involuntary squeak of delight, to find she was being watched by an open-mouthed woman in an expensive coat. Lucas's mum smiled weakly, put the pen and kiwi fruit into her trolley and headed for the checkout, leaving the woman staring after her.

The snow melted, the ice on the pavements receded and the trees dripped. Gradually, the temperature rose. One sunny morning in March, Lucas's Mum was depositing a pile of old magazines in the shed out of the way, when she heard Nijinsky moving about in his box. When she lifted the lid, he retreated back into his shell, but all the same, the weather was mild and she judged that it was probably about time or him to wake up properly. Gingerly, she lifted him out of his box and carried him into the house and into the living room, where she placed him on the carpet, near the radiator. Lucas took great interest in all this, as a precedent for Penghui's awakening, and lay on the carpet with his chin in his hands, waiting for Nijinsky to start moving about, and occasionally tapping on his shell with a teaspoon.

'Leave him alone, Lucas,' said his mother. 'How would you like it if I bashed you on the head with a teaspoon to wake you up? You know what a grumpy-puss you are in the morning. Let him wake up in his own time. He's been asleep for months and it will take him a while.'

But the bottom lip started quivering and she gave up. Lucas continued to gaze at Nijinsky but deigned to let his mother take the teaspoon from him. She took it back to the kitchen. She was close to tears herself. She was going to have to tell Lucas the truth very soon. Once Nijinsky was up to speed, so to speak, and Penghui still inert, there would be no hiding it. The previous evening, she had asked Lucas's father for advice. He had not been very sympathetic.

'It's your own silly fault,' he had said. 'Whatever possessed you to say it was hibernating in the first place? It's obvious that it would lead to trouble.'

'It seemed innocent enough at the time,' she said.

'The boy's got far too much imagination as it is without you encouraging him.'

It may seem strange to say that their marriage was being damaged by a kiwi fruit, but it was pretty near the truth.

'I could say that it died whilst hibernating?' she ventured.

'And back up one lie with another. He's going to find out that kiwi fruit are vegetables eventually.'

'They're not vegetables, they're…'

But his acid look silenced her.

'You'd better tell him the truth as soon as possible. Only make sure I'm not in the house. The boy's a nervous wreck as it is.'

So she was on her own. She finished peeling the potatoes, took off her marigolds, and resolved to get it over with. Just at that moment, she heard him call her.

'Mum!'

Now what? He seemed very excited.

In the living room, Nijinsky was awake and had lifted himself up on his scaly legs, while his flat head with its black pin eyes and fixed reptilian grin, moved ponderously from side to side, like a robot scanning the carpet.

'Here goes,' she said, coming in with a few thicknesses of double pages from The Guardian and a shallow but quite heavy earthenware bowl, containing tepid water. She set the newspaper down on the carpet, near Nijinsky's questing head.

'Will he drink it?' asked Lucas.

'He will if you leave him alone. It's a been a very long time since he last had a drink. He'll be very thirsty. But he won't if you bother him, Lucas, and if he doesn't drink, he'll be poorly. Now promise Mummy you'll leave him alone.'

'Can I watch him? Oh look, he's pulled his head in.'

'I expect that's because he doesn't want to listen to us talking. He's probably like Daddy. He doesn't like people talking at breakfast-time.'

'But, how can he hear us without any ears?'

'You ask too many questions, monkey. Just sit on the sofa if you want to watch him. And don't try to make him come out. I had to stop you sticking a twig up his tail end last summer.'

'Yes, but...'

'Never mind, 'yes but'. Mummy has work to do. Now do try and behave, Lucas. Mummy has a headache.'

And she retreated into the kitchen, secretly daring to hope that Nijinsky's resurrection had taken Lucas' mind off the wretched kiwi fruit.

Back in the living room, Lucas had extended himself on his tummy on the sofa, with his head hanging over the end. Nijinsky was under close observation but from behind. Sure enough, when he judged the coast was clear, out slunk the tortoise's head and he began to crawl laboriously towards the water. Lucas had seen a film where camouflaged soldiers were crawling through undergrowth, propelling themselves by their elbows. Nijinsky's crawl over the pattern of the carpet reminded him of that, although his elbows were turned out the wrong way. In slow motion, Sergeant Nijinsky hauled himself to the watering hole, pulled himself with his claws over the low rim, and began to sip. Then, in slow motion, he disengaged himself from the bowl, rotated - just like a tank, thought Lucas - and urinated over the masthead of The Guardian. Then, he withdrew his head and limbs.

'Mummy, Nijinsky did a wee-wee on the paper!' shouted Lucas, pleased that someone other than himself would get into trouble.

With the patience that only mothers can summon, Lucas' mother returned with another copy of The Guardian, picked Nijinsky up and laid him on fresh newspaper, in a corner. Then she took an angle poise lamp from her husband's desk near the window, plugged it in, and she set the lamp head about two inches above the tortoise.

'You might not think much warmth would come from a lamp, monkey, but it will help Nijinsky readjust, you'll see. Soon, he'll be scuttling about, and then it will be time for him to go outside again.'

'Is he not hungry, Mummy?'

'Well, yes, probably, but his tummy is all-confused and he'll need to sort himself out. We'll try him with a bit of lettuce in a few days' time.'

Sure enough, later that week, Nijinsky applied himself to a heap of lettuce, cucumber and some shredded carrot with considerable concentration. Ever since he had returned to the world of the living, Lucas had not once referred to Penghui, and his mother cautiously began to allow herself to feel that the crisis had resolved itself in just the same way Amber's interest in Nijinsky had been deflected. Even her relationship with her husband had taken a turn for the better, and he was coming home from the office earlier in the evenings. Lucas seemed obsessed with Nijinsky and would watch him for long periods, even when he retracted into his shell.

Later, Lucas moved Penghui from his tin on the radiator in his room to his little blue dinosaur activity desk, and placed him underneath his batman lamp on a copy of The Beano. His father had The Beano delivered along with The Guardian and The Observer, hoping that his son would take an interest in the comic and that it would help with his reading. Of course, his mother knew that her husband ordered The Beano for himself, and had done since he was at university. Lucas had been largely indifferent, but the latest copy would serve a purpose now if Penghui needed a wee. Without saying a word, he had also taken a shell-shaped soap dish from the guest bathroom and filled it with water, placing it reverentially near Penghui, along with some Haribos.

However, nothing was said, and Lucas' mother took heart from that, and from the fact that Lucas appeared to have turned his attention entirely to Nijinsky and to the Lego Junior Police Helicopter Set his father had bought him.

She couldn't have been more wrong. Lucas was playing the long game.

One bright, clear morning, two days after Nijinsky had resumed feeding, and rhomboids of sunshine fell from the windows and onto the carpet, Lucas' mother said: 'I think we'll pop Nijinsky into the garden his afternoon, monkey. It should be warm enough by then.'

Like all small boys, Lucas had a strong sense of injustice. There was Nijinsky, under the coffee table, smugly asleep inside his shell. That very afternoon he would be zooming around the lawn, or plunging through the shrubbery, while poor Penghui lay upstairs, in an enchanted sleep more profound, and possibly more fateful, than that in which the Sleeping Beauty had been enshrouded. How to break the spell? Lucas reasoned that he had replicated the conditions in which Nijinsky had come back to life to the letter. He had been taken from his hibernation nest. He had been placed on paper with water close by. He had been set beneath a lamp. What had he missed?

He sat astride the broad arm of the sofa which he regarded as his horse. Being in the saddle was a good place to think. He noticed that a patch of light on the carpet had moved a little, from a cluster of roses to a flourish of dark leaves. He tried to catch the light moving but it was impossible, and yet, and yet…there it was, illuminating the next knot of pink flowers.

Suddenly, Lucas knew what he must do. It was to do with being downstairs. It probably had something to do with the carpet itself. It would remind Penghui of being outdoors.

Lucas tiptoed upstairs to his room, and with infinite care carried Penghui and the soap dish of water down to the living room, where he set them down in front of the french windows, at exactly the spot where Nijinsky had come back to life, just over a week ago. Then he lay down on his front, his chin in his hands, to watch the awakening which he thought must be inevitable, and imminent.

'Lucas!' his mother called from the kitchen. 'Come and get your lunch.'

'I'm not hungry, Mummy,' he replied.

'Don't be silly. It's your favourite. Tomato soup with croissants.'

'No really. I'm not hungry.'

'Lucas, I don't have time for this. Come in here this instant.'

Wearily, Lucas clambered to his feet, and slouched towards the kitchen, with a backward glance to where Penghui lay on the carpet. What if he woke up while he was having his boring old lunch? He would miss the most important moment in his entire life. And Penghui would feel so lonely, waking up on his own. And tomato soup wasn't his favourite anyway. Pizza was.

Anyway, he wasn't going to tell his mother anything. She would only spoil things. Grown-ups always did. He clambered up onto his stool at the brunch bar and tried to look as sullen as he could. He stirred the steaming soup around a few times and then sat there with his spoon dangling vertically from his right hand. In his left he clutched a croissant and he rested his head on his knuckles. There were buttery flakes in his hair and all over the bar.

His mother tried to engage him in conversation. He would be starting school in September. It would be really exciting and he would make lots of new friends. There would be all sorts of games and activities and Mrs Parry was such a sweetie. He would learn ever so much and might even achieve his ambition to run a Circus in Space.

Normally, this would have set him prattling about what kind of alien animals he would have in his menagerie and the feats his interstellar acrobats would perform. Today, however, he said nothing. He put the squashed croissant down, rubbed his hair into greasy spikes and continued to play with his soup, lifting a spoonful into the air and letting it splash into the bowl.

His mother hoped she was right about big school. Nursery school had not been very successful. Lucas, whilst not particularly unhappy, had seemed to prefer his own company. The friendly advances of other children had been rebuffed. He had splashed blue paint on Jessica Glenn's picture of her mother, which had been unintentionally scary anyway. He had filled

Charlie Vereker's wellies with sand from the sandpit and then tipped the sand over Charlie's head when he protested. Any reprimand from Miss Charig would be met with volcanic tantrums, and on several occasions she had been forced to ring Lucas' mother and ask for him to be taken home. These explosions terrified the other children and it was not surprising that they had begun to shun him.

'Lucas, will you stop playing with your food,' she now said sharply.

'I told you I wasn't hungry, but you wouldn't listen.'

'There'll be no petit filou for you, if you don't eat your soup. And look at the mess you've made. You really are an exasperating little boy, Lucas.'

'I don't want a bloody petit filou! I bloody hate them! It's you who thinks I like them. They're bloody horrible and bloody bloody slimy!' he screamed, hurling his spoon on the bar so hard that it bounced off with a clang into the sink.

'Lucas! I will not tolerate such language. Go to your room. How dare you?'

'I will NOT go to my room,' said Lucas deliberately, catching and holding her eye for the first time. Then he swung off his stool and bashed through the door into the living room his mother in pursuit.

Then they both stood stock still.

Nijinsky had crawled across the carpet and was eating Penghui.

He had about a quarter of him in his mouth lengthwise. The horny beak pierced the brown fur, exposing the jewel-green flesh with its little black seeds. Juice dribbled under the reptile's old man's chin. The beak pierced the skin again and the tortoise showed his repellent pink tongue and swallowed a little more.

Lucas screamed and screamed. Lucas would not stop screaming.

*****

Lucas is seventeen now. He has not spoken a word since Penghui was killed, though he still has screaming fits at intervals. At first the family tried to cope with this. Nijinsky had to be given away to a tortoise sanctuary in Kent, after Lucas had made several attempt to harm him, once with a hammer. Amber, who had not shown the least interest in him for months, was suddenly anguished about his departure.

Most of the time, Lucas lay on his bed staring at the ceiling, refusing to communicate in any way. If he came downstairs, he would stand at the french windows gazing into the garden, but could not be persuaded to go out. He would not make eye contact. He would either look away or stare right through your head. At first their GP maintained that his silence was the result of shock, a kind of post-traumatic stress disorder. It didn't matter that the trauma had been caused by a vivid imagination and was in itself ludicrous. It was nonetheless powerful. The good news was that it was almost certainly temporary.

It wasn't. Whatever was wrong with Lucas, the most alarming symptom was his refusal to eat. He would sit at the table with his hands in his lap, looking at nothing. If his mother attempted to feed him, he would whimper, or sob as if he were out of breath - sure prelude to a tantrum, if the food were not whisked away quickly. Fruit could not be put on the table, any salad with lettuce or cucumber would elicit a flare up, and, one evening, in a towering rage, he demolished a large apple pie with his fists. His parents surmised later that this was because the pie had reminded him of the tortoise.

It was not long before his dramatic weight loss - he had been a chubby child hitherto - persuaded the GP that he wasn't going to get better on his own, and he was referred to a children's mental heath clinic, and admitted for his own safety.

He was well-treated. The ward was clean and the nurses caring and committed. There was little that could be done for him in terms of therapy. How could you treat someone who would not speak? Progress was made with his eating, however, largely through trial and error. He would agree to eat porridge, in tiny portions at first, and then increasingly large portions, eventually with honey stirred in. Scrambled eggs were tolerated on occasion.

There had been setbacks of course. He had hurled a bowl of sago pudding at a nurse and had to be isolated on the occasion where he had attacked another child with a stick of celery.

The only time he had been persuaded to communicate, he drew a picture of a child, presumably himself, with ears and hair, but no facial features whatsoever.

And so he continued in this condition, until the age of sixteen, when by law, he had to undergo the transition to an adult institution.

There he is now, living on porridge and scrambled eggs, and sometimes marmite toast, a recent addition to his diet. He is treated well because he causes no trouble. He can dress himself and keep himself clean and he doesn't wander or get under the feet of the nurses. He doesn't need any medication because there is no known treatment for his condition. Unlike many of the other patients, he doesn't require sedation. He is often allowed to sit alone on a bench in the garden for the whole day. His parents, now divorced, rarely visit, and if they do, he doesn't recognise them.

On rainy days, he sits in the day room. The scenes round him are appalling. There is a man who keeps whispering to him that he has sex with flies. Another claims to be sexually attracted to the space shuttle and says that he wants to be a welding machine when he is released, which he always claims is going to be the day after tomorrow. One believes his penis is stolen by demons every night and replaced in the morning. One man sits in a corner, facing the wall, and keens all day long. Several are as dissociated as

Lucas, but that is because they are so heavily medicated. Most of these people are filthy and bedraggled and the room smells of urine, and sometimes vomit. Lucas is oblivious to all this.

Lucas rarely has tantrums now. If he could tell you, or wanted to, Lucas would say that he feels unreal, as if he is watching himself in a film. Everyone around him is a stranger. His surroundings are different every day. He doesn't recognise his image in a mirror. He is waiting patiently for the day when a giant tortoise will arrive and release him from his internment, by ripping apart his green flesh and eating him.

Duck

[1979]

How long I'd been sitting there staring at the newspaper cutting on my desk, I couldn't say. It was, after all, a very long time ago. I remember that I'd used it as an excuse to get out of the rugby match that I was supposed to play in that afternoon, that I'd gone up to my study in the Old Wing and that I'd been gazing at the cutting since lunch when my father's letter had been handed to me.

I don't even remember much about my study now except that I'd covered every available inch of wall space with a collage of theatre programmes and advertisements from magazines, and that the mullioned windows gave out onto the playing fields, with the town and its spires beyond them, and in the distance the grey-mauve ridge of the Malvern Hills. I do remember the hissing of damp logs on the fire, which it was my privilege as Head Boy to have. Yes, that's how long ago it was.

And I remember clearly the muffled yelps and bellows from the remote pitch where the game was being played. I remember the dance of sunlight in the branches of the old chestnut outside my window, whose fat sticky buds would shake out leaves any day now. I remember watching the stately progress of immense flat-bottomed clouds piled high with dazzling froth. There was something about this spring afternoon which put it outside time.

My father had included no letter to palliate the brutally factual cutting, which stated that my cousin Seth, who had been serving in Northern Ireland, had been killed together with a young officer, when a booby-trapped car had exploded on a country lane in County Armagh. That afternoon, I felt neither anger nor grief. It would be a few hours before it hit me. I broke down so completely at Seth's funeral in Yorkshire that I was sent to Italy for three months and missed my last term at school. I think my father wanted me out of the way. Any show of emotion embarrassed him.

I hadn't seen Seth for nearly nine years. We hadn't been close in any ordinary way, yet for weeks I was sick with weeping and sleeplessness. On this first afternoon though, I felt absolutely nothing, apart from the curious suspension of time I have tried to describe and a kind of placid remoteness from everything.

I was turning over and over in my mind what had happened the last time I'd seen Seth. I think I must have been about eight. Ever since I could remember, Seth had come down from Yorkshire to spend the greater part of every summer with us at our home in South Wales. This year, for the first time, he had included me in his walks over Carn Fawr, and together we had watched the farmers' dogs rounding up sheep, built dams in the streams, lit fires and cooked sausages. Twice we had rescued a sheep entangled in the brambles. The first time we found it, it was so badly caught and panic-stricken that in its reckless dives into the thicket it had torn off its own ears. That's how we recognised it when we found the silly creature ensnared again, and Seth had dubbed it 'Lugless'.

I was rather in awe of him. Though we had spent most of every day in each other's company that summer, we were hardly friends. It wasn't just a question of our difference in age. I suppose he must have been about fifteen then, tall for his age, and thin like a hothouse plant, and I was ten, or maybe eleven, and quite small. Seth was fiercely independent, aloof and sulky, and he gave me the impression that my company was tolerated rather than enjoyed. Often he was gleefully and gratuitously cruel to me.

*

The clatter of crockery filtered up to my study. Tea was being laid out in hall for the rugby teams. At the end of a corridor was the bathroom where someone was running a bath and the pipes, which ran the length of the wing began to gurgle. I could hear again the little stream which ran past our house and down the valley. The impatient bubbling filled the nights and invaded my dreams. Again the wind moaned around my father's house, the owls hooted, the dog fox barked. In the bunk bed above me, Seth turned in his sleep and, after a while, his breathing regained its comfortable rhythm. In the mornings, he would awaken me by shaking the bunk bed, and I would open my eyes to see his lean brown arm hanging over the side of the bed and two fingers waving at me. Or, while I slept, he would pull back the mattress and spit onto my face from above.

I remember his last few days with us with especial vividness. We were making our way along the track the cattle had made through the bracken, along the flank of Cat's Hill. Iridescent puddles had filled their deep hoof prints and the muddy ground made the going all the more difficult. The early morning sun had produced a wash of brighter colours creeping to meet the line of shadows caught in the sunlight, and spiders' webs hung like shreds of lace from the gorse bushes.

'Shut up, will you!' Seth whispered angrily. 'You're making more noise than a herd of bloody elephants.'

'Sorry,' I muttered.

'Chuffin' shut up then.'

What with trying to keep pace with Seth's loping stride, trying to keep the busy brown flies out of my eyes, and trying to avoid the brambles which threatened to lash my eyes into pulp, it was hardly surprising that from time to time I had trodden on a twig. I began to feel put out. It was all very well for him: *he* could see where he was going. Several yards ahead of me he waded through the bracken with the shotgun across his chest. I could quite see that the sharp report of a snapping twig would disturb his concentration, but all the bearings *I* had were the buckles of his cartridge belt fastened on his hip. He made no concession to my age or my height, and tense as he was with excitement, he must have wished that he'd left me down at the house. I trod on another twig and nearly tripped.

'Lift your ruddy feet up, you div,' Seth said, between his teeth.

I stopped walking and quivered with indignation. I was almost ready to announce that I was going back to the house. I obviously wasn't wanted. It wasn't fair at all. Seth was being a hypocrite. He'd been treading on twigs too but, oh, that was different wasn't it? Anyway it was the first time I'd ever been shooting. How was I supposed to know what to do? And sloping off with my father's gun without asking frightened me. If Seth hadn't dared me, I wouldn't have come.

But I didn't say any of this, and when he turned and spoke to me again his tone was quite different. His hushed voice breathed of *shared* excitement, real complicity.

'Come here and keep down,' he said.

He was lying on his front against a bank, at the top of which was a natural gap in a sparse hedge. I crept up and lay beside him. The spot was just at the limits of my father's land and I knew well enough what lay beyond. There was a pond half-hidden in a beech copse, its bank soggy with last year's leaves and its margins choked with reeds and rushes. The bank was deceptive though, for on the other side the pond lay several feet below. Leading down to it was a steep face of solid rock.

'Listen,' Seth whispered.

Sure enough, I could hear duck. Seth stood up abruptly, stuck the butt of his gun into his shoulder and angled it. As I scrambled up the bank so that I could see, two ducks rose from the water with a rush of wings. Seth aimed at one of the birds, which was just gaining speed as it flew at a shallow angle over a clump of gorse. And then he swung the gun round at the drake. Perhaps his eye had been caught, as mine had, by the brilliant colours of the male's plumage, the purple-blue in his wings and the deep green of his head. Or perhaps he had calculated that here his chances were better, for the bird was rising vertically and so slowly that it seemed almost to be in slow motion. Rising like this, its breast was exposed and I had the feeling that I could distinguish individual fawn-grey breast feathers.

Though there could only have been moments between our first sighting of the duck and the shot, I seemed always to have been waiting for the crack. Even so, it filled me with a sudden exhilaration which I knew to be Seth's too. The duck's wing folded and it plummeted into the reeds. Seth turned to look at me, and his large brown eyes brimmed with astonishment and delight.

'I got it,' he yelled. 'What a shot!'

This delirium was short-lived. I had noticed movement amongst the reeds where the duck had fallen. It had not been shot dead and was struggling with one bloody wing outstretched. Seth had seen it too.

'Come on,' he said, and we scrambled over the bank and down a gully in the rocky slope to the patch of reeds. Seth was there first, and for the moment he stood immobile, staring at the poor flapping thing. It was no longer some abstract quarry, still less could it be thought of as food. It was a living creature in mortal fear and this close it was even more beautiful. As I walked up slowly, the bird moved his head and I was looking directly into his brilliant black eyes. I looked at Seth for some indication of what I was to think or feel.

An expression of pure brutality suddenly distorted his features and, with one movement, he brought down the butt of his shotgun on the bird's head. I fought down a mounting panic as the stricken thing lifted its head again. Seth picked it up by the wing and began to kick its head as dark blood started to seep from its beak.

'Die, you bastard' he yelled as he kicked. 'For Christ's sake, die!'

He dropped it on its back. It paddled its legs, opening and closing its beak, stiffened, slowly dropped its head to one side and was still. Seth kicked the duck over again and we both stood and stared at it. His eyelashes were wet.

*

I looked up from the blurred picture of Seth on the newspaper cutting. It was curious how little he'd changed: the dark blond hair, fair complexion, large eyes, reluctant smile. The neat moustache was different, of course, and the uniform, and perhaps his shoulders were broader. The sun was setting now on a cushion of dark clouds and the West was barred with gold, salmon pink and grey. The rugby teams were returning, caked with mud, and somehow I could tell that we had won. Four or five boys were well ahead of the rest, kicking the ball back towards the pavilion. 'Pick it up,' someone shouted. I started.

*

'Pick it up,' Seth had said.

'I daren't.'

44

'Pick it up,' he said, in exactly the same flat tone. Whatever excitement we had shared had ebbed.

'Why don't you?'

'I'm not touching it,' he said. 'Just pick it up by the feet.'

Gingerly, I lifted the duck up. It was still warm.

'It's heavy,' I said.

'Did you see it?' Seth said, ignoring me. 'What a brilliant shot!'

'What are we going to do with it?' I asked.

'We're taking it home, stupid.'

'We can't.'

'We're taking it home. We can eat it.'

'What'll my Dad say?'

'I don't care. We're not leaving it here.'

'He'll know you've had his gun.'

'Of course he'll know. What do you think I am? Thick?'

And he strode off. I brought up the rear carrying the duck. Four of five drops of blood dripped from the bird's beak onto my trousers and blackened into beads.

Whether Seth had calculated what our reception would be, or whether my father was uncharacteristically genial that morning, I don't know, but there was not the tempest I had expected. My father had a violent temper that sometimes belied his otherwise generous nature. Once – I forgot the offence – he had pushed me into my room and, tripping on the edge of the frayed carpet, I had knocked myself out on the leg of my bed. When I came to, he was cradling me in his arms and crying.

On this occasion, however, he was clearly torn by concern about the abduction of the twelve-bore and pride in his nephew's prowess with it. Seth was given a half-hearted lecture about the dangerous potential of the thing, the folly of taking me with him and the fact that it was illegal in any case.

'And if I catch you with it again, I'll make your arses glow. Now go and saw some wood, the pair of you,' he said, and he went to hang the duck in the barn. As soon as his back was turned, Seth gave me a wink.

I slipped out to look at the duck that evening. It was tied by one leg to the rafters and turned slowly in the beam of my torch. It looked eerie but I had no feelings about it now that it was dead. Nor did I feel anything but a purely objective interest the next day, as my father spread it across his knees and plucked it, the down flying all over the room. Even when he laid it out on the salting tray outside, cut off its head and legs, and pulled out the slimy length of yellow-green intestine for me to see, even then I only felt slightly squeamish.

The next day we ate it, stuffed with orange segments. Seth wouldn't touch it, and my mother cut him a couple of slices of ham.

Two nights later, we were playing on the swing on the slope of Cat's Hill. Seth had climbed nearly to the top of a tall solitary ash the previous summer and tied a rope to a strong bough. I sat astride a thick knot at the bottom and Seth pushed me out above the valley. At the highest point in my heart-quelling arc, I was sixty feet above the ground. I threw my head back to accelerate the swing and the sky, with its thick incrustation of silver, wheeled above me in an intoxicating rush. Later, sitting by the fire we had made near the foot of the ash, we shared a cigarette while Seth pointed out the Plough, the Little Bear, the Seven Sisters and the curve of Leo's mane. Then we sat and speculated in silence on the number of stars in the Milky Way.

After a while, Seth spoke. 'We're getting up early tomorrow,' he said.

'Why,' I asked.

'We're going after the female.' It was typical of Seth to speak like this, as if I didn't have any choice in the matter.

'Where?' I asked.

'On the pond.'

'How do you know it'll be there?'

'I saw it yesterday.'

'Dad'll kill you.'

'He won't. Are you coming or not?'

I didn't dare refuse. If Seth left me behind this time, he would never ask me to come out again.

'We'll get up about six. Bang your head on the pillow six times before you go to sleep.'

The next morning Seth and I were both awake before sunrise.

'Are you awake?' he whispered, after I had been lying there for a quarter of an hour, wondering whether or not the expedition was still on.

'Yes,' I answered.

'Come on then. It's ten past six.'

As we fumbled in the dark for our clothes, I felt a sharp pain in the joint of my little finger and a violent feeling of nausea. It was a moment or two before I realised what had happened. We had known for some time that the old stone chimney in our room harboured a colony of bees. For the most part this caused us little concern: we were only ever bothered by the occasional bemused and rather dusty visitor. I must have put my hand on one which had settled on my trousers and it had stung me. As I rubbed the spot, I let out a cry of pain, for I'd only succeeded in crushing the poison sac in the sting and injecting another spurt of venom into my finger.

'Shut up, you idiot,' Seth said.

'I've been stung, Seth,' I said.

'So what? Don't be so soft,' he replied. 'Come on, get dressed,' and he left the bedroom and crept through to the kitchen.

When I joined him he had a little paraffin lamp and was furtively making coffee by its feeble light. The cold grey haze of dawn was creeping up the valley and, as I stood shivering by the kitchen table, I examined my swollen finger.

'Come here,' Seth said as he stirred his coffee. 'Let's have a look at it.'

I showed him my finger.

'Does it still hurt?' he asked, though not very gently.

'Yes,' I murmured.

'It'll go numb in a minute. Then it'll wear off. Think about something else.'

So much for sympathy. In ten minutes we were clad in warm jackets and had pulled on our wellies. Seth took the gun from the corner and took a handful of cartridges from the box in the broom cupboard, where my father obviously thought they were safely hidden. As we left the house, we heard my father turn in his sleep and mutter something but then everything fell silent again and we made our way up to the pond.

As we pulled ourselves up the bank a little later, the sun was just climbing above the horizon, turning the mist down the valley into gold-tinged floss. If there were anything on the pon, it was giving us no warning. Again I felt the peculiar thrill watching Seth clutch the gun. I could see his index finger caressing the safety catch and, again, his tension communicated itself to me. If he was normally a little angular and ungainly, he was now lithe as a cat.

Whether or not I had managed to walk there more carefully than last time, Seth hadn't said a word since we left the house. He was infinitely cautious and we lay there for an age, perfectly still. A random gust of wind rustled the hedge and a flock of crows rose out of the fir wood along the crest of the hill. Only as they settled irritably did Seth stand and, at the same moment, I heard the whirr of wings on the pond.

As he stepped forward, the better to take aim, a hidden tentacle of the brambles on the bank caught at his ankles and, as he fell headlong, the shotgun leapt from his grasp. I gained the crest of the bank in time to see the gun slide down the rock, bounce off a ledge, spin in the air and, landing on its butt, strike the rock once again. With a report whose volume surprised me, although I had known it must happen, it went off, and I thought I saw an orange tongue of flame at its muzzle.

Almost immediately, the echo rang out on the woods over the Carn Fawr. Grating the rock as it went, the gun slid the last few yards into the pond.

Already high in the sky, the duck was beating her wings more easily, her long neck stretched out with unassailable grace. Seth lifted his head and groaned. There was a cut on his cheekbone. As he pulled himself to his feet, I pointed mutely at the spot where the gun lay in the muddy water.

'Well, get it then,' he said.

This made me angry. The injustice of a couple of weeks' complete domination hit me all at once.

'You dropped it,' I said. 'You go and get it.' It was the only time I'd ever contradicted him.

He seemed surprised, and then he grinned.

'All right then. Come on. We'll need a long stick.'

We scrambled down and fished the gun out without much difficulty, although it was in a terrible state, covered with mud and strands of algae. Seth rubbed it as clean as he could with handfuls of couch grass, but it still didn't look too good. Silent and dejected, we made our way back to the house to face the music.

I doubt if my father would have reacted so violently, if it hadn't been for Seth's attitude. He walked in airily, and had nothing apologetic about his manner at all. My mother was shopping in the village and my father was eating breakfast. He didn't say anything at first, but I knew his silence was dangerous.

'I dropped the gun in the pond,' Seth said. 'I know how to clean it.'

'Now that's hardly the point, is it Seth?' my father replied, still ominously quiet. 'And *you* ought to know better,' he went on, looking at me.

55

'He wasn't there,' Seth said quickly, before I could reply. 'He was playing on the swing. He only saw me on the way back.'

I was both gratified at this unexpected protection, and yet stung by the dismissive way he'd said it.

'I think you and I had better go and have a word in the barn, boy,' my father said to Seth, and they went out, my father telling me to go to my room. I don't think he believed Seth. I wondered what he meant to do. Surely Seth was too big to be beaten. I lay on the bottom bunk, straining to hear what was going on.

It was bad enough.

I could hear voices raised in anger, and then I distinctly heard Seth swear at my father. I'd never heard anyone swear in our house before, although Seth was pretty foul-mouthed when we were out on our own. My father was clearly furious. Then I could hear bangs and rattles, as if a scuffle were going on.

After a few moments, Seth burst into the bedroom, pulled his suitcase from under the bed and haphazardly began to throw in his clothes. He was flushed and close to tears, although he wasn't going to cry in front of me.

'What did he say?' I asked.

'He's sending me home. I've got to pack and then he's driving me to Aberystwyth to put me on the train.'

'Why?'

'I don't know, do I?'

I knew this wouldn't have happened if my mother had been at home. It was all out of proportion.

'Did he hit you?' I asked.

'No, I pushed him. He fell in the wheelbarrow. I think he's broken his glasses.' This was accompanied by a grin of satisfaction.

When Seth had packed, we went through to the kitchen where my father was waiting. One of the lenses of his spectacles had been temporarily repaired with sellotape. Not a word was said as he held the door open, and Seth went out with his suitcase. My father followed him and I was left alone.

I had been sitting on the kitchen table dangling my legs for five minutes or so, when the door burst open and Seth appeared very much out of breath.

'I said I'd forgotten my toothbrush,' he panted. He threw a pound note on the table. 'Here. Don't say anything. Get yourself some spice,' and he was gone again.

*

Sitting in my study in the gathering gloom, I wondered how I had spent that pound. It would have been some comfort to know now. It was nearly dark, and the only light came from the fire as a glowing log shifted and flared up briefly. From below, where the boisterous rugby teams were having tea, a discordant victory song floated up to my study. I'd almost certainly spent the money on sweets, as Seth had suggested. I was crying and shivering now. I never saw Seth again.

Even through my tears, I could see that there was no logic to my grief. We had exchanged no letters: there had been no contact of any kind. I had been touched by his parting gesture, and it had been brave of him to take all the responsibility for the gun, but how many more memories there were of his teasing or bullying me, of nights in the bunk bed beneath him, lying miserably awake thinking over some jibe deliberately meant to hurt. Yet I felt there to be a tenuous connection between that long timeless afternoon at school and the tantalising moment of suspense before Seth fired at the duck. I couldn't get out of my head the image of him fighting back tears when the creature was dying in pain because he hadn't shot it dead. Somewhere, not in my head but in the integuments of my heart, beyond logic, there was a link between the wounded bird flapping in the reeds with its helpless wing outstretched, and the blood and charred flesh and splintered bone that had been found near a burnt-out car the previous morning, on a windy road in County Armagh.

Just a Little Kitchen Supper

Of course, I hadn't wanted to go in the first place. The invitation had filled me with foreboding as soon as it hit my inbox. 'Just a little kitchen supper,' Perdita had written. 'There's someone I'm dying for you to meet. And you know how Roger loves your company.' God, she's trying to marry me off again, I thought, and as for Roger liking my company, well, I'm afraid there's no way I can reciprocate that. Roger is the kind of bloke who doesn't just shake hands but grabs your forearm and works it up and down as if you were the village pump, whereas Perdita will only allow you to take the tips of her fingers because she thinks it's more ladylike. There is a certain shock beyond the arrogance of it. It is like touching a halibut blindfold.

Roger tells interminable anecdotes about the month he spent in Japan eighteen years ago, and when you laugh at what you think and hope is the punchline, he carries on, because it wasn't the punchline, and there probably isn't one anyway. If you attempt to tell a beautifully turned story yourself, just as you reach the tersely witty climax, he will pull his smartphone from his pocket and say, 'I'm sorry, I just have to take this' and when he's finished his call, he'll say: 'Sorry about that, where was I?' and we're off to Fukuoka again. Perdita has only one topic of conversation, her two precocious children, Joachim and Jasmyne-Jayde.

So why did I go? Not through any sense of enduring friendship, I can assure you, though Roger and I had hung out together a bit at university and Perdita had been mildly amusing before they married. Not through a sense of duty or obligation either. None of that stuff. No, it was partly because I am constitutionally incapable of dropping someone even if they've long become tedious and irrelevant. It's a tiresome weakness this excess of politeness and has cost me many hours of boredom. However, the principal reason was shame.

Three times I had cried off, once with a fictitious near mortal toothache, once because I claimed to have confused the dates ('You know what I'm like,' I'd feebly improvised) and once because I said I'd been called to an urgent business meeting in Scunthorpe.

'But, Miranda Oliphant said she saw you in West Hampstead Waitrose yesterday,' said Perdita, who telephoned me the following day. Damn, why hadn't I waited for the answerphone to kick in? Yes, some of us still use a landline.

'Good Lord, I must have a body double,' I squeaked, with a silly little giggle that quavered with mendacity and panic.

'You must have,' Perdita sniffed, making it clear she didn't believe a word of it. 'So what about next Saturday evening instead?' She was deadly in her persistence. You had to give her that. And unbelievably thick-skinned with it.

'Yes, yes, of course.'

'Seven-thirty for eight?'

'Oh, yes, fine. I'll be there. Definitely. For sure. Absolutely.'

So there I was stuffed and trussed like a chicken.

Their invitation was a return fixture, you see. They'd been to dinner at my flat a month or so before, hard though that may be to believe after what I've told you. Roger had phoned me one evening.

'Luke, old man, you'll never believe it, but Perdita and I have just moved into a house just down the road from you in Cleve Road. We must meet up, you old rascal you!'

It was true. I lived just the other side of West End Lane, not five minutes away.

'We must indeed,' I said, feigning enthusiasm.

'When is to be, me old china? Few beers at The Railway?'

I detest pubs.

'Why don't you and Perdita come over here for dinner?' I heard myself saying.

I could have cut out my own tongue, boiled it, and served it up with capers and anchovies.

I had meant it as one of those nebulous invitations that get put on the back burner till finally the gas goes out but Roger pounced on the idea with alacrity and there was no way out. A date was fixed for the following week and I set about making the best of it.

I pride myself on my cooking, you see, and I thought that if I put an impressive meal on the table the evening might be marginally less tedious.

I served up warm figs stuffed with gorgonzola cheese, on a bed of rocket, with a port wine sauce, and Perdita shut up about Joachim's Kumon maths lessons for a whole minute to ask where I'd bought the figs and what was in the sauce.

The main course was my pièce de résistance: Beef Wellington: a fat fillet of beef, red and glistening at the centre and oozing its sublime juices, coated with a duxelles of wild mushrooms with a splash of madeira, topped with foie gras and encased in heavenly puff pastry, creamy, light and pale gold, decorated with pastry leaves. From it arose a savoury steam. It was perfect. I placed it on the table as a midwife might place a new-born baby on a spotless towel.

Perdita was touching up her lipstick in a pocket mirror. Glancing over the top of it, she said: 'Oh, I can't eat that, Luke. I'm sure I told you I'm a veggie.'

Resisting the temptation to ram the entire thing down her cleavage, I served Roger, and quickly confected an omelette, resolving never again to let these absurdities over my threshold.

However, here I was, outside their huge house on Cleve Road, trying with little success to control a resentment which kept rising like a very nasty acid reflux. The house is a hideous Victorian monstrosity, with ostentatious castellations, pinnacles and turrets and two round windows on the first floor which, from the other side of the street, make the whole tasteless edifice look like an immense Gothic owl, warty and demented.

This effect is enhanced by a pair of miserable yew trees which stand sentinel on either side of the risibly huge front door with its great hinges and iron studs, a portal which would only be proportionate if it gave access to a cathedral. Here, it just looks daft, though it does stand appropriately as a metaphor for Roger's ego.

Clutching a 2000 Pauillac, I squeeze between a dusty Renault people carrier and an immaculate, blindingly white BMW and tug at the ornate door pull. It comes away in my hand and distant bells jingle indoors.

Roger throws open the heavy door and takes the wine from me with one hand, though it is in the crook of my arm and I haven't proffered it, and with the other he relieves me of the medusa-headed door pull.

'Don't worry about that, Vieux Fromage,' he says genially, 'it's always doing that. 'Meet Joachim and Jasmyne-Jade.'

'Bonjour,' says the girl fixing me with a gaze of stony appraisal and extending a hand whose tiny nails have been painted a shiny amethyst, though she cannot be more than four years old.

'Bonjour,' I say non-commitally. She has been taught to offer only her fingertips by her mummy.

'Wie gehts, Luke?' says her sly-faced brother, who is maybe a year older.

'Well, precisely,' I reply, astonished at the impudence of his using my forename though I have never met him in my life before. 'I couldn't have put it better myself.'

'Don't you speak German?' it sneers incredulously. 'In this house, we speak French in the morning, German in the afternoon and English in the evenings.'

I look at my watch with what I hope is a sardonic flourish.

'Really, well, according to my, no doubt antiquated, timepiece, it is 7.43 pm BST, and so, if it is perfectly all right with you, I shall reserve the right to use the vernacular, and you must forgive me for not being a polyglot.'

'What is he talking about, daddy?' says the infant diva.

'I say, Old Stick, easy on the sarcasm,' Roger says, placing his hairy hand on the child's neck. 'They're only kids.'

Suddenly, Perdita descends upon us from nowhere, like a harpy on speed.

'Luke, darling!' she squeals, air-kissing me with an alarming noise, rather like a plunger liberating a particularly tenacious blockage in a kitchen sink. I hate this. One cheek, two - oh, dear-lord-and-father-of-mankind - she is going to go for the full three because she thinks it's French. Inevitably my specs get tangled in her hair and our noses are somehow compromised. I am nearly gassed by her cloying scent.

There is something very wrong about this. What happened to the frigid fingershake? Why this effusiveness? Then I get it. Perdita Navenby-Gore is quite drunk. And what is more extraordinary, there is the sour tang of tobacco on her breath though this is a woman whose position on smoking is close to Nero's on Christianity.

'Luke, how could you do this to me? I said six o'clock on the dot, you naughty man. Everyone has been here for absolutely ages. Roger, where *is* Nanny? Do sort out the children for me. Nighty night, darlings. I'll pop up for a kiss later. Luke, there's someone you simply have to meet.'

Can you hear me screaming? I am trying to internalise it.

There is no point in attempting to protest. I let her drag me by the elbow through a hallway that has been *designed* to look untidy. I mean it. There are green wellies in an artful line in descending order of size, with the last one consciously toppled over. There is - dear Jesus - an elephant's foot umbrella stand containing not just brollies but canes with brass and ivory handles representing grotesque heads, serpents, crocodiles and all manner of ghastly tweeness. There is a more than life-size native American Indian carved from wood and crudely painted, past which only one fairly slender person could squeeze at a time, and beyond it, a rocking horse, golf clubs, skis and an ironically retro collection of telephones in primary colours. There are even Lego bricks scattered on the cleverly distressed parquet. Why?

We pass through a door with glass panels in the style of William Morris into an attractively overgrown garden. There is a mulberry tree in the centre of what was once a circular lawn though now the grass has grown to ankle length. There are meadow flowers in it, cornflowers, buttercups, poppies, cow parsley, and a couple of very tall thistles.

'The Garden!' she announces, as if I were in danger of mistaking it for the bus station. 'I do so hate those trim little gardens with their herbaceous borders and their petunias. So bourgeois, darling, don't you agree?'

I say that I think the artful neglect is very charming but do not mention the crass decking and white plastic garden furniture which lie at the bottom of the garden beyond the mulberry tree. The other guests are standing there chatting and holding glass cups of what I think might be yellow bile.

'Try this!' beams Roger, who has miraculously materialised down here without passing us, having presumably dealt with Nanny and the whelps. He ladles some of the yellow broth from a large Victorian chamber pot into a glass cup and comes towards me. 'It's called Fukuoka Punch. I invented it myself.'

I'll bet you did, I think, taking a tentative sip. It is powerful, medicinal and very nasty.

'What's in it? I ask.

'My Old Flugelhound, you do not want to know!' And he begins to hoot until he is almost breathless, looking round at the other guests for support. I am very embarrassed.

But he's right. I don't want to know, though I detect sake, pastis, banana Sambuca, and dry ginger ale in the noisome mix. There are sliced bananas bobbing in it, pointlessly. Now, I know why Perdita is squiffy.

'Roger! Will you stop monopolising my lovely Luke!' she shrieks and grabs my elbow in a pincer grip. 'Come and meet our new friends,' she says, manoeuvring me towards the others. I have just time to put my punch cup down (I hope forever) on a retro, glass-topped table, quite at odds with the plastic furniture.

There they stand, in a semi-circle, around the chamber pot, a tableau-vivant of people I know, at first sight, that I would never have *chosen* to meet. There is a terribly thin woman in a kaftan, with twiggy arms and wholesome sandals, with (yes) live flowers braided into her very orange hair, an ageing wood nymph whose sunken eyes and thin pink lips scream 'needy'.

There is a young American, about twenty, shaven till he shines, wearing a dark three-piece suit, a crisp white shirt and a pale blue tie. He looks so clean that if you were to touch him he would squeak.

I am introduced to an Australian drama teacher at one of the new universities. He is hobbit-sized with a mane of white-hair, round glasses, opinions, and PROJECTION. His sandy-haired leading man and boyfriend is perhaps twenty, tall, and as floppily loyal as an Afghan hound.

I am also introduced to an octogenarian literature don in a crushed cream linen suit and a loose pink and white striped bow tie. He is from Corpus something or other, from one of the posh places. He fixes me with a look that suggests hostility (I don't want you here), disgust (I don't want to be here myself), and collusion (You don't want to be here either, do you?). He is smoking greedily right down to the stub. He has very small, square, yellow teeth and a watery eye. I think he might be wearing a wig. There is a damp stain in the crotch of his trousers though he smells of a very expensive toilet water.

'But it's *Annabelle* you must meet, darling,' Perdita squeals. 'I just know you'll get on like a house on fire, you two,' and I am physically whisked around to face Annabelle.

'Oh, you two!' Perdita purrs holding her clasped

hands up to her mouth as if at a basket of puppies.

Annabelle is a full six inches taller than I am with the shoulders of a rugby forward and thwacking thighs to match. I don't know quite why I said 'thwacking' but the word comes to mind at first sight of her and seems the *mot juste*. It even *sounds* like the *mot juste*. She wears a severely masculine white blouse, a beige suede skirt and terrifying leather boots. She has an Eton bob of shiny blond hair, big blue eyes and – well – features that could be quite pretty, if you could sort of persuade a sculptor (here he is, quaking) to approach her and kind of massage her face into a - you know - *smaller* version. As it is, I am thinking warily of those gigantic female spiders who eat their mates after copulation, though copulation is not part of my current (or future) plan. She holds out her hand and I expect to have mine crushed to powder, but no, I get the halibut.

On the other hand (as it were), I notice that she is wearing a wedding ring. Perdita leaves us conspicuously alone but together. There are long pauses in the conversation. No, I don't keep ponies. Yes, I've lived in London all my life. No, I didn't go to public school. Did *you*? Oh, you went to Benenden, did you? That's unsurprising. What do I mean by that? Oh nothing, nothing.

Very long pause.

'You're married, then?' I venture, really, really wanting to confirm this, so I can put an end to Perdita's matchmaking.

'In a manner of speaking.'

'Oh, really?' (I am clutching at social straws here) 'What does your husband do?'

'He's in the RAF.'

'Oh yes, where is he based?'

'RAF Scampton in Lincolnshire.'

'Ah, I know Lincolnshire well. There's some beautiful countryside up in the Wolds, isn't there?'

'It's a shithole.'

'Ah.'

Interminable pause. I try again.

'Have you done anything exciting this summer? Done anything interesting?' I am wilting internally with the warm-lettuce feebleness of it.

'Just got back from climbing in Nepal.'

'I say, that's remarkable. Was your husband with you?'

She turns on me.

'Why do you keep going on and on about my husband, you ridiculous little man? He's just left me, you silly interfering fool.'

And she stalks off, through the meadow and round the mulberry tree and off to the house.

'Oh, Luke! What on earth did you say?' whines Perdita from the tableau around the chamber pot as Annabelle slams the garden door.

'I but... I... but look I didn't... no,' I burble inanely. The other actors in the tableau look at me as if I'd just reached up Annabelle's skirt and given her knickers (surely tweed) a furtive tug.

'How could you?' Perdita wails. 'Annabelle is my very best friend. I just wanted everyone to be happy and now it's all RUINED!'

She sits down hard on the glass-topped table which shatters with a loud crack. Perdita is left sitting on the ground among the shards, with her legs hanging ludicrously over the metal frame. One calf is bleeding. The chamber pot has overturned and the sticky yellow brew is seeping into the decking.

There is a frozen moment as everyone looks down at her, her face a rictus of shock. Our embarrassment seems to ripple out across the meadow in waves. And then, rather horribly, she begins to laugh. True, there is a smack of hysteria in her laughter, but I think she is doing it to show us what a good sport she is. Some of the creeps begin laughing with her.

Roger hoists her rather unceremoniously to her feet. She is a sorry sight. Her silver and purple cocktail dress is splashed with guacamole and taramasalata, and batons of carrot and celery are stuck to it. Most of the Fukuoka Punch has landed in her lap. There is a vast unseemly stain and the vile stuff is dripping from the fringed hem of the dress. Perdita holds her arms out, away from her body, and bursts into noisy tears.

Roger shakes her elbow a little and turns to the rest of us.

'I'm afraid dinner is going to be delayed a little, people,' he says. 'Do talk among yourselves, won't you?' And then to Perdita, 'Come along you, let's get you changed.' And he marches her off like a naughty toddler, she still sobbing inconsolably, gasping for breath.

People look at their shoes for a while.

'Tell me,' says the wood nymph to the don (who has lit another cigarette from the stub of his last one), 'are you happy with the choice of a woman as Poet Laureate?'

'And a Sapphic to boot?' replies the don, one eye half-closed and watery in the smoke he has just exhaled. 'Well now, what you must understand about poetry and the establishment is that…'

I am out of here, I think, in that rather apt locution of the young, and I inch, invisibly, I hope, away from the group towards the meadow, where I subject the mulberry tree to a very thorough inspection.

Bits of conversation waft over: 'Gerard Manley Hopkins' ablutions…polysemic ineluctability…Augustan coprophilia…in the Tory DNA…Ruskin's potty training…therapy---mumsnet…Leavis…from cradle to grave…'

The tree is a fine specimen, in fact, and obviously very old, its roots rising out of the mound in which it grows like the crooked legs of an enormous and malign spider. Some of its branches are so gnarled and wizened that they are propped up on forked struts, reminding me of nothing so much as certain paintings by Dali where atrophied limbs are similarly supported. There is something unsavoury about this tree. All the same, the leaves are fresh and healthy and fruit is beginning to appear although the berries are still a greenish-white and not the rich purple they will later become. I remember reading somewhere that the bark and the unripe berries are mildly toxic, stimulating or hallucinogenic. Might it be possible to space myself out of this disagreeable gathering by snaffling a few mulberries?

I am just about to drift over and join the clutch of pseuds on the decking when more fragments gust over on the summer breeze: 'Bit standoffish, isn't he?...Don't know him from Adam...Old flame of Perdita's I think (I wince as one does at a hypodermic needle, realising rather late and lamely that they are talking about me)...Pal of Roger's from uni, I believe.'

Now, I may not have been to one of the toff joints, but I have sufficient dignity and years to cringe at the word 'uni', nasty little import that it is. Be that as it may, I quash the urge to stride over and correct these aspersions and find I am suddenly wildly fascinated by the patterns in the mulberry tree's bark. If necessary, later on, I will pass myself off as a botanist.

But there is only so much scrutiny that a mulberry tree will bear and it is an absurd kind of mercy when Roger appears at the garden door, beaming as if nothing has happened. He is holding, I blush to say it, a Victorian gong. Perdita is by his side in a red and gold cocktail dress which reveals a great deal of her rosy bubbies. She too is grinning like the cat in the adage. Roger strikes the gong with aplomb, ghastly drama queen that he is.

'Dinner is served,' he says plummily, as expected.

The sycophants actually break into applause as they wander towards the house. I follow them at a distance, mute.

Close up, Perdita is not as refreshed as she appeared from a distance: the eyeliner on one eye is approximate and her lipstick is slightly smudged in the corner. Her smile seems appliquéd too.

'Now then, my dears and my darlings,' says Roger, giving the gong a little shimmer, 'let us put that little mishap behind us and begin the evening proper. Perdita, my treasure, lead the way.'

'Now, people,' she says, 'I had thought we would eat in the kitchen – much more friendly, don't you think, but Roger made such a frightful mess preparing the dessert that we are going to have to eat in the dining room which we hardly ever use.'

'Pardon, lady, pardon,' croons Roger in mock reverence.

'Come through, everyone,' says Perdita leading the way to the front of the house. I have to admire the way in which, given the evidence that she is several sheets to the wind, she manages to retain her crisp alpha-mother diction.

We turn into the dining room. It is unspeakable. The walls have been painted a deep purple colour, while the woodwork, skirting boards, dado rail and cornices are glossy black. There are two enormous gilt mirrors, with flowers and writhing cupidons. The silvering of both is tarnished in places and the glass of one of them is cracked (conceivably on purpose). From the rather high ceiling hangs a grotesque bronze chandelier with translucent globes of a bilious yellow. Around the table, there is an assortment of chairs, all different: a kind of stage throne is at one end in front of black double door; there is a rocking chair at the other; there are couple of carvers; a fake Queen Anne chair; a child's school chair, piled high with assorted cushions; a white garden chair and a bar stool. The table is laid with similarly multifarious and garish crockery and cutlery and the smallest wine glasses I have ever seen, some of them clearly very expensive but all minuscule. There is a great green Victorian vase of overblown lilies in the middle of the table which is lit by a number of Victorian oil lamps some of which are smoking toxically, their glasses becoming greasy and blackened on the inside. It crosses my mind that Roger is using the wrong kind of oil, though I am no expert on that kind of thing. The whole room is a temple to kitsch.

There is one redeeming feature, however. The oval table (which I know will wobble) is laid with the most exquisite tablecloth. It is of gold silk and embroidered with the most gorgeous birds, peacocks and parakeets and birds of paradise, amid palm fronds and other great tropical leaves. There are great clusters of oranges, limes and lemons. There are canteloupes and tamarinds and little bright red berries, sharp as drops of blood. It is quite, quite beautiful.

I say so to Perdita. It seems like the first thing I have said in hours.

'My great grandmother made it. It was handed down. Isn't it simply lovely?' she says, and for a moment she looks like a girl again and I almost feel sorry for her, seeing in the moment how delightful she could have been had she been allowed to be genuine.

But in the end, the moment cannot annul the horror – nothing can negate the horror beyond horrors - for there, sitting in the seat to the left of the throne is Annabelle, seething like a stock pot.

'Now, Luke,' says Perdita with sickening inevitability, 'won't you sit here by me?'

'By me' means to the right of the throne, opposite Annabelle, who snorts like a Grand

National winner. I give Perdita a look that would curdle cream, a look as tart as a gooseberry.

'Ah, maybe not,' she says, with uncharacteristic sensitivity. 'To *Roger's* right, I meant. I'm sure you two boys have *so* much to talk about. No, Dale, you come and sit with us. I know you and Annabelle will get on swimmingly.'

The immaculate young man with the dark suit and the one kilowatt teeth approaches and Annabelle looks at him as if he were an amuse-bouche.

And so, between them, Roger and Perdita have us seated and I learn their names. Of course, I was told before who they are, when we were introduced around the fatal chamber pot, but I was not paying attention then. Now, it seems necessary, because we are going to be stuck together for another hour or two, unless some kindly earthquake or charitable hurricane should split us asunder. Opposite me, is the pre-Raphaelite wood nymph, Mandy, at least thirty years beyond her credibility date. Next to her, is

Jeff, the booming drama teacher, and to his left and Perdita's right, Shannon, his fluffy quivering boyfriend. To my right is Cottesloe, the literature don. I do not know if this is his surname, some sort of inflated forename or some kind of academic sobriquet, but it seems to suit his self-importance. Sandwiched between him and the still simmering Annabelle is Dale the hygienic American, whose teeth are like beacons declaring: 'Give me, your huddled masses, yearning to breathe free.' It is hard not to take offence at his self-assurance.

Now, when all are seated, some comfortably, some precariously, and Jeff on a chair so low he barely reaches the table, Perdita says: 'Now do get to know each other better, won't you? I think the first course, should be ready by now. The recipe did say "resist the temptation of peering into the oven", so I'm a little nervous. Still, fingers and toes crossed, eh?' And she gives a nervous little laugh, bordering on hysteria. Then, with her smiling mask re-applied, 'Roger, the wine.'

'Ah, Perdita, you don't mind if I smoke in the house, do you?' says Cottesloe.

'Of course I mind, you outrageous little man. I don't know how you even dare ask.' She stands indignantly. Roger rushes to her side.

'Now, now darling, come along,' he says, ushering her through the double doors into the kitchen. I note that she is trembling with rage. Over his shoulder, Roger says to Cottesloe, 'Best not, old boy, best not.' And he closes the doors behind him.

Silence takes command in the dining room. Everyone seems utterly stunned by Perdita's extravagant and disproportionate mood swing, but to tell the truth, I am not, and have been expecting something like it for a while. It seems Cottesloe is unimpressed too. He produces a crumpled packet of Benson and Hedges, takes out a slightly bent cigarette, lights it from a rolled silver cigarette lighter, draws on it deeply, squints at each of us in turn, gets up, and without a word he leaves. After a moment, we hear the heavy front door bang shut.

The silence thickens until it is just too embarrassing. Mandy and Jeff speak at the same time.

'Did I tell you about the time I went to Assisi?' flutes Mandy. 'I met this adorable nun who plays the mandolin. Well, I sing you see, and we thought we should get together and form a duo. We were going to call ourselves Sorores. That's Latin for sisters, you see, but her Mother Superior...'

'Shannon, I think you should tell everyone about playing Juliet at the Uni Theatre,' drawls Jeff. 'Obviously, he's made for Romeo (look at the bone structure) but we thought it would be good to do an all-male production to draw attention to LGBT issues. It's going to be set during a feud between two rival breweries in Blackburn, so we had to rewrite the prologue and...'

'Oh, I'm sorry, do go on,' says Mandy, feeling out-talked.

'No, no, no, you go on – it sounds fascinating,' says Jeff.

'No really…'

'No, I insist…'

During this pantomime, Dale turns the full beam of his teeth in my direction.

'Do you think we could take advantage of these few moments for me to talk to you about Our Lord, Jesus Christ?'

You can feel my innards twisting can't you?

'Er, well no,' I bluster, 'because, you see, it would be pretty pointless, because, er, you see, I'm…er…Jewish!'

About as Jewish as a Norfolk piggery, as it happens. But it is no use. My venial little lie is trumped.

'But so was Jesus!' cries Dale in triumph, his teeth as radiant as the face of God.

I am saved, if not from damnation, at least from further attempts at proselytising, by the reappearance of our host and hostess. Roger throws open the double doors with a flourish and

Perdita appears bearing a tray with nine ramekin dishes on it.

'Where's Cottesloe?' she says immediately, and the ramekins slide perilously on the tray.

'Gone,' says Shannon with all the anguish of Juliet in the Capulets' tomb.

'Home,' I clarify, lest Perdita should think he has taken poison or stabbed himself. 'Gone home.'

'The bastard!' says Perdita darkly.

'I say, steady on, Princess,' says Roger, 'you never really liked him.'

'Yes, I did,' she cries. 'I did so. It was you that called him a rancid puffball!'

And then, first Roger, and soon Perdita, begin to giggle and snigger.

This is a bad sign, I think.

'Shitake Soufflé!' Perdita announces shrilly. I now see that Roger is wearing oven gloves which represent Punch and Judy. He takes a ramekin and places it delicately in front of each of us, whisking away his hands, like a concert pianist who has just played some majestic chord.

'They were perfect when they came out of the oven but they do seem to have collapsed a tadette,' says Perdita ruefully.

This is to understate the case to the point of deceit. They are sorry things. The middle of each one has sagged almost to the bottom of the ramekin and the edges of most are burnt.

'And seconds for one lucky person!' says Roger, placing Cottesloe's portion on the black marble mantelpiece where it will doubtless remain till the crack of doom. 'Now for some wine.' He disappears into the kitchen.

'It's made with Lapsang Souchong,' says Perdita over-precisely. Has she been topping up in the kitchen?

'What? The wine?' This is me, surprised now at nothing that happens in this household.

'No, silly! The soufflé!'

Roger returns bearing aloft one of those carafes you used to see everywhere in the seventies. You know, Paul Masson's California Red, I think it was called. Looked and tasted like dilute Ribena.

Roger turns it around. Hopping Buddha, it *is* Paul Masson's California Red. He peels off the foil cap and pours the stuff into the doll's house glasses. No sign of my Pauillac, or anything any of the other guests may have brought. Unless, one of the other guests *did* bring this. Dale perhaps? In which case, Roger's stinginess is even more crass.

'Eat, drink and be merry, for tomorrow we die!' he roars. Just at the moment the latter proposition seems the more appealing.

We try to eat the soufflés, each in our own way. Perdita pokes at hers with her fork but doesn't actually eat any, and in the end, she dangles her fork listlessly from one hand, whilst her head rests in the other like a neo-classical statue of Melancholy. Unnervingly, she is scrutinising the rest of us. Jeff and Shannon prise bits from the ramekins as Jeff regales us with further tripe about the Lancastrian Romeo and Juliet. Surprisingly, Dale and Annabelle are deep in conversation, heads inclined to each other like lovers. They too manage only the occasional forkful of collapsed stodge. I cock an ear. Ah, they are talking about horses, not Jesus. Mandy has given up on her story of the nun with the mandolin as she struggles courageously with her portion. And Cottesloe has gone. Home.

The soufflé is truly appalling. It has the texture of chamois leather, though with probably less savour. There is something inexplicably slimy about the mushrooms and then I keep finding tea leaves sticking to the tip of my tongue. Tea leaves. I can see that the Lapsang Souchong was supposed to add a smokiness to the dish but surely the recipe asked her to add an infusion to the egg mixture not for her to bung in a handful of leaf tea. I manage to finish it somehow. It's all down to that damned congenital politeness I told you about.

All the same, Roger devours his with apparent relish. I marvel at him. Is this in support of his wife? I think not. Is his palate so crass that he cannot tell that this is a crime against gastronomy? Maybe. I have a mental picture of Roger in a red leotard with blue stars mechanically devouring razor blades, light bulbs, nuts and bolts.

'Yum!' he says. 'Jolly well done, darling.'

Incomprehensible.

'Now, more wine, anyone?' Roger is on his feet.

Well, of course, they want more wine, Roger. You've scarcely given them any. I haven't touched mine, however, because I know quite how nasty it is. So when Roger comes to me, I put my hand over the glass, half expecting him to pour anyway, in time-honoured music hall fashion. Fortunately, he doesn't or I would have had to hit him.

'Something wrong, old sparrow?' he asks. 'Seem to remember you never turned down a glass of the old vino collapso at uni.'

This is a vile slander. I may have to hit him anyway.

'Lent,' I say.

'Lent is in February, friend of my youth. It's nearly September.'

'Just a joke, Roger.' I drop my voice to a conspiratorial whisper. 'Doctor's Orders. Bit sensitive.' I can feel my nose growing.

'Oh rightio. Yes, I see. Say no more. Nuff said.' He turns to Perdita. 'Shall we clear, me deario?'

This time Roger holds the tray as she bangs the ramekins onto it, chewing her lower lip the while.

'That was gross and you know it,' she mutters savagely.

'It was delicious, my poppet. Now, don't make a fuss,' Roger replies, smiling through clenched teeth, and once again he ushers her into the kitchen. There is much banging and rattling and now there appears to be a heated argument going on, although we can only hear individual words such as 'mortgage', 'career' and 'my precious children', strain as we might. We are like children who fall silent in class whilst another child is being screamed at by a teacher in the corridor. There are a few gutter expletives too.

Then, the kitchen is silent, and we begin to chatter, anticipating the flinging open of the double doors.

Their next entrance is indeed quite melodramatic. I have to give them credit for showmanship if nothing else. Once again, Roger throws open the doors to reveal Perdita holding a huge china platter on which sits a capacious copper mould such as one might see in the kitchens of Hampton Court or Burleigh House. It is ribbed and domed like the mother of all party jellies.

There is one discordant note to all this pomp. In the corner of Perdita's mouth burns a forgotten cigarette. Though she is smiling, her eyes seem unfocused,

'Mesdames et Messieurs,' proclaims Roger, with a French accent I would place somewhere near Leighton Buzzard, 'my wife's *chef d'ouevre*: Layered Vegetables in Aspic featuring: carrots, asparagus, aubergines, peas, tomatoes, mange-touts, courgettes, butternut squash, and pimentos, red, green, yellow, orange, and black. And here, in this crystal vessel – 'He holds up a glass jug. ' – is a basil and tomato coulis for your delectation.' He places it on the beautiful tablecloth.

If she has pulled it off, this should indeed be a most attractive dish, the vegetables in colourful strata inside a shimmering tumulus, like jewels under viscous glass, tart but laced with sweet white wine.

'And now*, tantantara*! - the lovely Perdita will reveal her culinary marvel!'

'You do it, Roger,' says Perdita in a strange, shrill voice and she sits down rather suddenly at her place.

'Certainement, mon alouette,' he says. 'Esteemed guests, attend and mark.'

There is a copper ring in the top of the mould and Roger takes hold of it. With a flourish, for Roger does everything with a flourish, he lifts the mould clear of the serving dish.

The savoury jelly docs not hold even for a second. It collapses at once into a gelatinous gloop studded with vegetables mixed promiscuously in a meaningless slew. The dish has quite deep lips and most of the substance is contained although some is beginning to ooze onto the tablecloth.

Perdita moves with unexpected speed.

'Hell's teeth!' she shrieks, 'That took bloody hours.'

She picks up the platter with both hands and hurls it violently at one of the grotesque mirrors on the wall. The result is apocalyptic. The great gaudy thing drops to the floor and the glass shatters into splinters which join the shards of the serving dish on the black-lacquered floorboards. I can see from the larger ones that, when whole, it had bccn a rather tasteful piece of *chinoiserie* with a riverside scene in maroon, blue and gold.

A large patch of glistening slime begins to run down the purple wall.

Wailing extravagantly, Perdita rushes out through the doorway into the hall by which we entered, closely followed by Annabelle who turns at the door and bellows darkly: 'Damn you all! Look what you've done to her now! You men are all the same!' which leaves poor Mandy totally bewildered, yet looking unaccountably guilty.

We are all standing now, muted by shock and awe.

Mandy moves to pick up some of the crockery and glass.

'LEAVE IT!' booms Roger, and then more benignly, 'leave it Mandy. The cleaner will deal with it in the morning.

'Sorry folks. I'm afraid I could see that one coming a mile off. I think she'll probably go to bed now. She's been under a lot of stress lately. Thinking of changing therapists.

'But don't let us allow this little tantrum to spoil our evening,' says Roger blandly, as one might turn from watching the mushroom cloud at Hiroshima back to a bridge game, saying 'shall we play another rubber?'

'Perhaps we ought to go,' Jeff ventures.

'Won't hear of it, man. Won't hear of it. Sit yourselves down. You cannot possibly leave without sampling **my** contribution to the feast. That would be churlish wouldn't it?'

Roger makes the invitation sound like a threat. Annabelle returns looking tragic.

'She's asleep.'

'There we are then. Sit down. Sit down. Come along. Why don't we all move to another seat. No, this end of the table. There, that's good. Now I am not going to be a moment.' And Roger disappears behind the theatrical doors.

Fearing another protracted silence, Dale says, 'Mandy, why don't you tell us about your singing nun?'

'Oh, no, it's not really that interesting.'

'Sure it is.'

'Yeah, Mandy, tell it,' pleads Shannon.

So Mandy resumes the lugubrious tale of the hippy and the nun with the mandolin, but before Jeff offers to write the screenplay Roger appears again, this time backwards. He comes through the double doors buttocks first, carrying a tray.

'Now, when *I* create something in a mould, it does not collapse. Turned these out in the kitchen and they are purr-fect. Meine Damen und Herren, crème caramel!'

He places them on the table and to my surprise they look wonderful. There are two. One in the shape of a cat – ah, Roger, I see what you did there - and the other a motor car, both very stylized. The crouching cat has pointed ears and the huge eyes of a thirties cartoon cat, while the car has rounded doors and high rounded wheel arches. The moulds were surely art deco design, probably found somewhere in Camden Market.

We applaud politely. Yes, even I put my hands together.

'Impressive, Roger,' I say. It is possibly the only compliment I have ever given him.

'Fanks, geezer,' he says in an atrocious attempt at a cockney accent. 'They're not from a packet, you know.'

If this is true, then he has done very well. The custard is the palest of yellows, and the caramel which coats the top of the car and the cat's head and back is dark and lustrous. They have been turned out of their moulds deftly and even the tricky points of the cat's ears are precise. The texture must be just right.

'And now,' says Roger, who is not going to be upstaged by his own creation, 'for the finishing touch, I give you crème caramel flambée!'

No! Roger, I scream inside my head, don't ruin the only edible thing that has been put on the table the whole of this purgatorial evening. Roger, please, I'm starving.

But Roger is not telepathic and I am unheard. He produces a copper ladle which has been stuffed down the belt of his trousers and from a pocket comes a bottle of cognac which he passes before us like a conjuror. He pours some of the brandy into the ladle and begins to heat the base with a cigarette lighter, circling the flame around the bowl to heat the brandy. I watch intrigued. This is a preposterous idea but his showmanship is mesmerising.

When he sees the brandy begin to fume, he ignites it and in the low light we can see the blue flames dancing over the liquid which he pours over the car and there it is, burning eerily.

'And now the cat,' he announces. 'Don't tell the RSPCA.'

He pours more cognac into the ladle.

No, Roger. That's too much, Roger. But I don't say it.

The brandy heats more quickly this time since the ladle is already very hot. He ignites it and pours it over the cat, this time from a greater height for even greater histrionic effect.

The cat is alight but there *is* too much brandy and it spills still flaming over the serving plate and onto the beautiful, beautiful tablecloth where it scorches a hole and the edges continue burning.

Roger reaches over to try to put it out with a napkin but knocks over one of the Victorian oil lamps. The fuel spills out and catches fire. The blaze on the table is serious now. We stand back stunned. Annabelle rushes towards the kitchen for water but Dale intercepts her.

'No! You don't pour water on an oil fire.' And he moves to take his jacket off to beat out the flames.

But Roger is faster. He rushes to the other end of the table and in one last, furious conjurer's gesture, yanks the tablecloth towards him and behind him onto a sofa in the bay window. However, his flamboyant gesture only sends another of the oil lamps to the foot of the opulent drapes up which bright flames begin to rush. Within moments, a rim of bright flame appears on the seat cushions of the sofa and it too goes up. Black smoke is rising and rolling along the ceiling.

Screaming and shouting, the others are trying to beat out the flames with whatever they can find.

Unnoticed, I slip into the kitchen. It is in a dreadful mess, used pots and pans and bowls and plates and utensils and ingredients all over the place. In the midst of the chaos, however, I espy my bottle of 2000 Pauillac, unwrapped but otherwise untouched. I pick it up and slip through another door into the hallway and thence to the heavy front door. As I turn to close it, I see Perdita, Joachim and Jasmyne- Jade, hammering down the stairs shrieking.

As I squeeze between the BMW and the 4x4 into the drive and out onto Cleve Road, I seem to see black silhouetted figures moving against flickering yellow and orange light in the bay window, like some strange Japanese shadow play from Fukuoka.

I have some Saint Nectaire cheese at home which will go nicely with the claret.

Come Away, O Human Child!

Come away, O human child!
To the waters and the wild
With a faery, hand in hand,
For the world's more full of weeping
than you can understand.

W.B.
Yeats

The first child disappeared in Lincoln, just outside M&S. He was about six. Sporting trainers with flashing lights at the heels, he had spiky black hair and a button nose. Without a word of warning, he let go of his mother's hand, swivelled as if he had been turned around by an invisible touch on the shoulder, became two-dimensional like a playing card, and slipped, like

108

a posted letter, into a crack between the paving stones.

During the course of that morning, over four hundred boys and girls, all under ten, vanished in the same manner, slipping into cracks in the pavement as if they'd been filed away. A colourful group of laughing, babbling, primary schoolchildren, walking in pairs alongside the Brayford Pool with their beaming teachers, suddenly vapourised into a thin mist, were wafted over the water, and were then rapidly swept up into the slipstream of a flight of swans. In the afternoon, a baby girl, being baptised in the cathedral, turned into a sparkling golden liquid, which poured out of the christening robe of ivory lace that had been in the family for eleven generations into the ancient black font. There she promptly evaporated and was never seen again. At evensong, the younger choristers were lifted by their surplices, like tufts of thistledown, into the air under the vaulting. Then, with the softest of detonations, they were all extinguished, except for two trebles, a boy and a girl. These two soared in a glorious kyrie above the nave, spiralled and shivered into a multi-coloured glitter, which floated up into the high tower at the crossing, and then, growing ever fainter, was breathed out through the grotesques on the south side of the Minster, there to dissolve in the hot tremulous air of the city's traffic.

Over the next few days, the disappearances spread throughout the county.

In Louth, babies in buggies turned into fluorescent, soapy bubbles, which swirled around for a few moments, reflecting all the colours of the High Street. Then they burst, leaving only a little dampness on the plastic seats. In Skegness, all the children of the town atomised at once, and the mist swirled unnoticed around the legs of the tourists and the phlegmatic donkeys, to be whisked by the bracing wind, out over the North Sea. In Cleethorpes and in Mablethorpe, they just dissolved into the warm sea fog, like sugar in tea. At about the same time, all the children of Boston sublimated into a rushing cloud of steam which rushed just above the surface of the ground to Boston Stump, where they were sucked up the spiral stone staircases and exhaled invisibly into the air.

Within a month, all the children of the United Kingdom of Great Britain and Northern Ireland had vanished, sliding into the pavement, melting and leaking into lawns, sucked up into great public monuments, or swept along the surface of the Severn, the Tyne and the Thames in a coruscating, chromatic haze. Within a year, all but one of the children of the world were gone. They were hoovered up by twisters in the American Midwest; they dried out in the Australian Outback and fell to the ground in a dust so fine that it was invisible; in India they were simply washed away by the monsoon, and in China, the whole child population swelled the mighty torrents of the Yellow River as it rushed through the Nine Provinces and emptied the children's mingled atoms to dissipate in the Bohai Sea.

The remarkable thing was that nobody noticed, or seemed to mind.

For a long time, things carried on much as they had before. Young mothers still wheeled their pushchairs up and down the High Street, blocked the narrow aisles of HMV, and parked them in clusters outside Starbucks, but they were quite empty. Some residual maternal instinct still had them plumping pillows and adjusting covers, but there was no one there. People still bought Pampers and baby oil and jars of baby food in an automatic sort of way and then just stored it away. Schools still opened and teachers taught classes to empty classrooms, while management continued to create ways of occupying their time, with surveys, training, questionnaires, briefings, inspections, scrutiny and meetings. Whether the lessons improved in quality in the absence of the children was a moot point. It was certainly quieter. Paediatric wards were quiet too. The beds were immaculate, their hospital corners crisp and razor sharp, but there was no-one in them. All the toys were tidied away and the nurses had time to work on creative displays and to gossip at the nurses' station. The paediatric consultants were moved to geriatrics or to administration.

There were effects on the economy, of course. After a year or two, the British Government, whose civil servants seemed to understand what was happening only in terms of balance sheets and cost-benefit analysis, began to phase out child allowances and family tax credit, along with maternity and paternity payments. People were still having sex, of course, with even greater enthusiasm and inventiveness, but no new children were born. A kind of global amnesia ensured that this loss of fertility went unremarked. Divorces rates tumbled in the West. In China and India, and in Africa, the population explosion was halted, steadied, and went into reverse. In the United Kingdom, for several successive years, the Chancellor of the Exchequer, beaming from ear to ear, was able to hold up the battered red box outside Number 11 on budget day and announce fabulous increases in the state pension. Older people were not only granted bus passes for life but free and unlimited rail travel too. From November to February, the state would now pay all fuel bills to people over fifty-five years of age. As people began to retire earlier and earlier, teenage unemployment was unlocked. Expensive salaries no longer paid out to ageing employees turned into comfortable job opportunities for the young. Youth crime figures plummeted. It felt like a golden age.

There were unexpected consequences as there always are in a change of the weather, of demography, or diet. There were no children to zoom around pubs unreproved by indulgent parents, who had been used to treating licensed premises like a crèche. No longer would they bribe their offspring with sugary drinks and crisps to go and bother others and get under the feet of beleaguered waitresses. In fact, women began to forget about pubs altogether. Gastropubs died. The day of the Slug and Lettuce was over. The Rose and Crown, the Royal George, the William IV, and the Eagle and Child returned as the proper preserve and refuge of men. True, the breweries became less interested in decor and soft furnishings and bars quickly re-acquired a certain dinginess. Menus dwindled again to cheese and ham rolls, pie and peas, and, inexplicably, pickled eggs made a reappearance. Teenagers still had their noisy clubs, of course, with their sticky carpets and vomit-splashed toilets, but eventually there were no more teenagers.

Rail travel became infinitely less stressful.

During these years, many people noticed that a strange and compelling figure was putting in appearances around the globe. He was first seen in the Arboretum in Lincoln leaning against the ornate bandstand. He wore a straw hat stuffed with feathers and fresh flowers which never seemed to fade, a white shirt with voluminous sleeves, over which were two sashes, one green and one red, black breeches with a blue cummerbund, white stockings and black, dusty brogues. Around his upper arms there were bands with many silver bells and on his braided gaiters there were many more. His face was blackened with boot polish. He carried a tabor, on which he tapped a mesmeric beat, and on a little silver pipe, he played a warbling melody somewhere between the song of a blackbird and the gargling of water as a bath empties. He would be seen talking to the winos in the green metal shelter under the monkey puzzle tree and then he would dance for them, the bells jingling madly. All the while, he wore a fixed, thin-lipped smile.

In no time at all, it seemed, social websites reported sightings of an identical man, sometimes in widely separated places, simultaneously. Photographs were posted of him dancing outside the High School in Morristown, New Jersey; in the public gardens in Hamelin, Western Australia; outside City Hall in Lincoln, Nebraska; at the University campus in Pipertown, Saline County, Missouri; outside Le Petit Tambour Hotel near Calais, and outside the Maison de Champagne Piper-Heidsieck in Rheims. He was seen in Poland and Lithuania, Mexico and Lesotho, and always with the same thin-lipped smile. He never spoke except to vagrants and to the inebriated, who, later, could never remember anything about the conversation. No-one could discover anything about his identity.

Now, round about the time the last teenager turned twenty, people began at last to miss the missing children. It may have been because they had become bored with themselves or it may have been because colour began to leach from the world. This happened infinitesimally slowly so that no-one quite believed the evidence of their own eyes. It was as imperceptible as the slowest imaginable fade to black in a theatre. For two months it went unremarked, just like the disappearance of the children. The sky took on the colour of dirty linen and the disc of the sun, when it was seen at all, became white. All depth of colour seeped from the fields, and the crocuses, when they bloomed, were the palest of pastels, and the trumpets of the daffodils were grey, not gold. Colour drained from the faces of people too, and before long, there were no more blue and green eyes, no flaxen hair, no cherry lips, no blushes. Not even cosmetics prevented the leaking of colour from the world, because the lipsticks, and powders and lotions all turned to variegated shades of grey. In the end, the whole planet became like an over-exposed black and white photograph from long ago.

Then it began to rain. It began to rain in April, and it hasn't stopped since.

Some blamed the bankers, many blamed the politicians. Some Christians blamed gay marriage, an epidemic of fornication and the ordination of women bishops. Other evangelicals muttered that the iniquity of the fathers was being visited upon the children unto the third and fourth generations. The Daily Mail blamed wind farms; The BBC and the press blamed climate change. The elderly would have blamed the young, had there been any young left.

The only splash of colour, a dazzle of red and blue, and yellow and green, in the whole ghostly monochrome world, was the man with the thin, obstinate smile and the jingling silver bells. The flowers in his hat were still fresh and vibrant and the feathers as bright as ever but he was seen less often, and no longer danced or played his pipe and drum. Instead, he was seen pushing a little boy in a wheelchair, whose wasted legs were in callipers. The little boy never aged or grew, but in his eyes was the heartache of the world for the loss of colour and the absence of children.

And then one day, as drab as any other, just outside M & S in Lincoln, England, the man went off. He went off like a Roman candle, sending out four coloured balls of fire pursued by white streaks of flame. One ball was crimson, one cobalt blue, one electric green, and one a dazzling white. These in turn burst into stars of golden sparks fretted with red ones like rubies or pomegranate seeds. The sparks showered towards the earth but faded and vanished in wreathes of smoke long before they could land. Instead, a couple of handfuls of tiny bells, suddenly struck the ground and bounced on the pavement, jingling as they rolled apart, and shortly afterwards, a bright blue cummerbund fluttered down and collapsed on the flags. The smell of burning lingered in the air.

The boy in the wheelchair wept softly in the rain, amid the astonished crowd. He wept for the playmates he had never had and would never have. And he wept for the man with the pipe and the tabor, and the flowers in his hat, who had left him behind and alone for ever.

Acknowledgements

Warm thanks to Jill Lormor for typing the manuscript of Duck, to Kate Turner for the proof-reading, and to Harry Gelder for help with formatting the cover.

Any remaining errors are my own shameful fault.

Printed in Great Britain
by Amazon